Ultimate
Unauthorized
Nintendo® Game Boy™
Strategies

Ultimate Unauthorized Nintendo® Game Boy™ Strategies

Corey Sandler
Tom Badgett

BANTAM BOOKS
TORONTO · NEW YORK · LONDON · SYDNEY · AUCKLAND

Ultimate Unauthorized Nintendo® Game Boy™ Strategies
A Bantam Book / June 1990

ISBN 0-553-34992-9

Published simultaneously in the United States and Canada

PRINTED IN THE UNITED STATES OF AMERICA

0   9   8   7   6   5   4   3   2

To Janice and Lynn, the powers behind the thrones.

Preface

The Nintendo Game Boy delivers a whole new world of fun to the palm of your hand.

Its designers have taken away a lot: the television set, the separate controllers, the power supply, the video converter and cables, and several pounds. But then they added stereo digitized sound and a whole passel of wonderful games. The computer chips inside the little machine are every bit as sophisticated—in some ways more so—than those that are within the full-sized Nintendo Entertainment System.

The tiny built-in screen of the Game Boy is its greatest shortcoming, and yet it may also be—in a way—a strong point. It is very difficult to play a casual game on the Game Boy. The tiny characters and the single-color graphics demand your total attention.

That's when we discovered what we call the Great Game Boy Grip. That is the tensed muscles, beaded brow and fierce grip of a player deep into a challenge. He or she throws hands, eyes, ears and whole body into the game.

We've also seen the Game Boy breathe some new life in some old types of games. You'll find in this book a collection of some real headscratcher puzzles, starting with Tetris, which is included with most Game Boy machines purchased. Tetris combines brainpower with fast hand-eye coordination; you'll also find slower, more traditional puzzles that will draw you deep into the innards of the Game Boy.

About This Book

Game Boy arrived in the U.S. market in the Fall of 1989, and was one of the bestselling games for the Christmas season of that year despite the fact that there were only four games available to play. The full stream of Game Boy titles only began to arrive in the Spring of 1990.

In this book, we have tracked down 41 of the most exciting titles in that first wave. Most of the games we worked with were not even completed as this book went to press; we were sent computer chips, temporary game cartridge holders and in some cases prototype game paks that were larger than the Game Boy they plugged into.

You may have to be a bit patient in waiting for some of the games we've written about; some are available now, while some of them will not arrive in stores until the Christmas season of 1990.

You'll find some heart-thumping challenges like Batman, Super Marioland, Motocross Maniacs, Paperboy, Skate or Die and Spiderman. You'll get to play super-athlete in competitions including Bases Loaded, NBA Basketball and Malibu Beach Volleyball. You'll meet Dracula in Castlevania, Bugs Bunny in Crazy Castle and Kung Fu Kid.

We're very proud to be delivering to you this third book in the Ultimate Unauthorized Nintendo Game Strategies series.

Our basic purpose is this: Before you spend $25 for a piece of gray plastic inside a closed cardboard box sealed in a sheet of cellophane, buy this book. We'll tell you the inside story.

We call this book series **Ultimate** because we think you'll find that the information presented here is more complete, better organized and presented than you'll find anywhere else.

It's **Unauthorized** because these books are not sponsored, endorsed or in any way approved or disapproved by Nintendo of America or any of the companies whose products we have written about. This does not mean that we don't talk to the makers of the games; it just means that we listened and then made our own judgments before sitting down at the keyboard to write the book.

We offer **Game Boy Strategies** because we think players want to earn their way to the end of the games. If you want step-by-step instructions, get a book on knitting. We want to help you use your own abilities.

We have come up with a standard format for all of the games we write about. This is the cure for all of those inconsistent and confusing manuals you find inside those sealed boxes. We think you'll find that the organization of each section—the same for every title—will help you quickly learn new games or new strategies for old ones.

At the top of each game writeup you'll find the Ultimate Game Flag. Here you'll find the following information:

The best age group for this game. We do this for two reasons: to help you as a player choose games that you'll enjoy, and to help parents select age-appropriate challenges.

We've also included a **Difficulty Rating.** This was a tough one to assign. There are some games that 7-year-old William Sandler can zip through but his dad can't get past the opening scene; there are some beginner's games that dad enjoys playing just to relax. Here are the categories:

Novice. You're new around here, aren't you? The first round of games for the Game Boy seem to be aimed just above this level, but we expect that sooner or later companies will deliver games for the very young for the Game Boy, just as they do now for the full-sized Nintendo Entertainment System.

Apprentice. You're able to leap tall buildings on the second or third try; earn your wings and develop your skills with these entertainments.

Hot Dog. What? 337 more Zizzer-Snagger Missiles? No problem! I've been there before . . . but, wait, wait . . . watch out? Aargh!

Master of the Game. Turbo powered games for supercharged players.

Inhuman. Where does the computer end and the player begin? These are the toughest of the tough.

The game category. It wasn't easy, but we've divided the games into 10 types:

 Aliens and Monsters. You'll meet—and fight—all sorts of weird creatures here.

 Amazing Quests. There are all sorts of princesses waiting to be rescued. You'll go eyeball to eyeball with Count Dracula, swing with Batman, stick to Spider-Man and fight wizards and warriors with Merlin in Gauntlet II.

 Car Wars. Drive yourself crazy in Motocross Maniacs.

 Flying Feet. Oomph! Aargh! Kick! Punch! Slash! Fight alongside the Kung-Fu Kid or challenge the Fist of the North Star.

 Fun Learning. Who needs a boob tube? Be the star all by yourself in Jeopardy or Wheel of Fortune!

Gym Bag. Are you in shape for Malibu Beach Volleyball? Ready to step up to the plate for Bases Loaded? Want to play a few frames of World Bowling?

 Just for Laughs. Break windows and get paid for it in Paperboy, or help a little tiny Mario rescue yet another unfortunate princess.

 Lost in the Maze. Exercise your mind and your fingers with clever and sometimes-maddening puzzles like Kwirk. Tetris, Flipull or Dexterity.

 Shoot-em-ups. Knock down the alien blocks in Alleyway or the alien space ships in Nemesis.

 Strategies and Simulations. Play electronic versions of some of the age-old great games such as Shanghai or Ishido.

 Video Link. Want to play dueling Game Boys? Some games now allow you to play against a friend, your Game Boys connected by a cable. For more information, see the "Video Link" section later in the preface.

About the Nintendo Game Boy

Pound for pound, or should we say ounce for ounce, the new Nintendo Game Boy is one very impressive piece of computing/game equipment.

It includes all of the features of the full-sized NES in its small package, except for the quality of the picture. The Game Boy, of course, does not send its image to a color television set but instead to its tiny (about 1.5 inch by 1.5 inch) built-in screen. On the other hand, the mighty midget Game Boy has full stereo sound output that makes the original NES sound like a scratchy record.

Here are the vital statistics for Nintendo's new Boy:

Born: 1989 in Kyoto, Japan.

Product Name: DMG-01.

Marketing Name: Nintendo Game Boy.

Weight: 10.5 ounces, with four batteries installed.

Size: 3.5 inches wide, 5.8 inches tall and 1.3 inches thick.

Power Source: 4 AA batteries, or rechargeable battery pack.

Electronics: Custom 8-bit CPU (Central Processing Unit) of CMOS design. CMOS stands for Complementary Metal Oxide Semiconductor, which is a design of electronic chips that draws very little power and therefore works well in battery-operated systems. Also included in Game Boy are two 64Kbit static RAM memory chips, used to store information about the game and screen image in progress.

Audio: Full digital stereo through the headphone jack. Monaural (one channel) sound through the built-in speaker. The speaker is automatically turned off when a headphone is plugged into the Game Boy.

Display: Liquid Crystal Diode (LCD) image, dark blue against yellow-green background.

The Screen

About the LCD: The screen in the Game Boy works by electrically charging portions of a matrix of tiny diodes, making them turn clear so that light can reach a dark background behind them. Images are made up of hundreds of tiny dots.

A television screen also produces its images using a "dot matrix" but the TV works by actually giving off light when the electron gun strikes a phosphor dot on the inside of the screen. The LCD does not produce any light, but instead reflects an image using the light that is around it.

You'll find very quickly that the Game Boy is best used when you have a strong light that shines on it at about a 45-degree angle. Be sure to use the contrast adjustment dial on the left side of the device to try to find the best setting.

The LCD is also fairly sensitive to extreme temperatures. If it is very cold, the LCD screen may become noticeably slower to respond, or even completely stop displaying an image. A very hot or very cold temperature could cause the LCD chemicals to change, destroying the screen. So, be careful not to leave the Game Boy out in the sun, in a particularly hot place like the inside of a car parked at the beach, or in a cold place.

Now, here's some Good News and Bad News: the designers at Nintendo have come up with an interesting piece of hardware that allows a Game

Boy cartridge to be displayed on a large television screen, just like the NES game paks. It's called the Wide Boy.

Here's the Good News: the Game Boy cartridge slips into a special holder that plugs into a Japanese Twin Famicom game machine that is attached to a TV set. The special holder allows you to add a background color to the screen, too.

The Bad News is this: first of all, the whole shebang is not intended as a consumer product, but instead is aimed to help developers of Game Boy games. Even if you could lay your hands on the whole package, you'd have to face a price tag of between $750 and $1,000.

But in any case, now you know how many of the video game magazines—and this book—produce their pictures of Game Boy screens. In the case of *Ultimate Unauthorized Nintendo Game Boy Strategies*, we used a Wide Boy plugged into a Twin Famicom that was plugged into a special computer video camera to produce high-resolution slides.

The Sound System

About the headphones: First of all, although the sound is quite good through the stereo earphones that come with the Game Boy, you don't have to limit yourself to that particular design. Any Walkman-like headphones with the same miniature plug will work—be sure the plug is stereo.

If you want the ultimate in Game Boy sound, here's a tip you won't find in the instruction manuals: Try plugging your Game Boy into your home stereo system!

First, you'll need the proper cabling and plugs. A visit to your local Radio Shack or other electronics store should turn up exactly what you need for under $10.

At the Game Boy end, you want an 1/8-inch stereo plug adapter that converts the line to two monaural phono plugs.

To connect to the stereo, buy a pair of six- or eight-foot phono "patch cables." (You can find in many stores a single cable that has two phono connectors at each end.)

(You may even find a specialty cable that combines both pieces in one: it will have a 1/8-inch *stereo* miniature plug at one end and two monaural phono plugs at the other.)

Now, *making sure that the power to your stereo system is turned off*, plug one end of each phono cable into an unused PHONO or AUX input at the amplifier or receiver. One cable is used for the Left signal and the other for the Right.

Plug the miniature stereo plug into the Game Boy and connect the cables together.

Set the amplifier or receiver's input switch on the front to PHONO or AUX (whichever you used), turn on the stereo system and the Game Boy and listen to the music!

The Video Link

About the Video Link cable: One of the really exciting features of the Game Boy is that it can be used in head-to-head competition with another system. This is not just a matter of two players taking sides in a single game—you can already do that in a number of NES games. Instead, with some Game Boy games such as Tennis, Baseball or Tetris, each player sees the game from his or her own perspective.

Here are a few basics of Video Linking:

1.   You must have two Game Boys.
2.   Each Game Boy must have its own copy of the game to be linked.
3.   You must interconnect the two Game Boys with the Video Link cable (one is supplied with each system purchased.
4.   Make sure that the power is off when the cable is plugged into each Game Boy.

The Batteries

About the batteries: You should get at least 10 hours of life from a set of fresh AA batteries; Nintendo claims as much as 30 hours is possible. The best type to use are alkaline batteries. Nintendo warns against using the cheapest carbon batteries because they may leak; the electrical characteristics of rechargeable nickel-cadmium batteries are not recommended either.

You will use up more battery power if you use the built-in speaker in the Game Boy. Some game paks—those with more internal memory—will use slightly more power than others.

When the power level of the batteries becomes too low, the battery light on the front of the Game Boy will become dim, and the sound through the speaker will become weak and slightly distorted. When you notice this, you should remove the batteries. A weak battery is more likely to leak or otherwise damage the system than fresh batteries.

Nintendo sells its own Rechargeable Battery Pack that plugs into the Game Boy. You can also expect other companies to offer their own battery packs for the system.

We Want to Hear from You!

Have you discovered more Ultimate tips you'd like to share with other players?

Join our panel of Ultimate Players and help us prepare the next books in our series. Send tips, comments and information about yourself including name, age, address and telephone number to:

Ultimate Players Panel
WORD ASSOCIATION, INC.
P.O. Box 6093
Holliston, MA 01746

And don't miss the Ultimate Players Newsletter offer at the back of this book!

About Volumes 1 and 2 of *Ultimate Unauthorized Nintendo Game Strategies*

We'd also like to suggest that you be sure to include copies of Volumes 1 and 2 of *Ultimate Unauthorized Nintendo Game Strategies* in your library. They'll tell you what you need to know about more than 100 games for the full-sized Nintendo Entertainment System. Here's a list of games in those books:

Volume 1

Adventures of Lolo; Air Fortress; Airwolf; Amagon; Bad Dudes; Bases Loaded; Bionic Commando; Blaster Master; Bomberman; Bubble Bobble; Bump' n' Jump; California Games; Cybernoid; Desert Commander; Double Dragon; Double Dragon II: The Revenge; Fist of the North Star; Flying Dragon: The Secret Scroll; Friday the 13th; Gauntlet; Goal!; Golgo-13; Guerrilla War; Hoops; Hudson's Adventure Island; Ikari Warriors II: Victory Road; Ikari Warriors I; Ironsword: Wizards & Warriors II; John Elway's Quarterback; Kid Niki; Knight Rider; Kung-Fu Heroes; Legacy of the Wizard; Mappy-Land; Marble Madness; MegaMan 2; Mickey Mousecapade; Milon's Secret Castle.

Also: NFL Football; Operation Wolf; Othello; Phantom Fighter; Platoon; Prisoners of War; R.B.I. Baseball; Rambo; Renegade; RoadBlasters; Robocop; Sesame Street 1-2-3; Sky Shark; Spy vs. Spy; Star Voyager; Strider; Super Mario Bros. 2; Super Mario Bros.; Superman; Taboo: The Sixth Sense; The Legend of Zelda; The Uncanny X-Men; The Guardian

Legend; The Three Stooges; Thundercade; Tiger-Heli; Ultima: Exodus; Uncle Fester's Quest; WCW Wrestling; Who Framed Roger Rabbit; Wizards & Warriors; WWF Wrestlemania; Zelda II: The Adventure of Link; 1943: The Battle of Midway; 8-Eyes.

The book includes previews of the following games: The Adventures of DinoRiki; All-Pro Basketball; The Battle of Olympus; Bigfoot; Clash at Demon Head; DuckTales; Genghis Khan; Godzilla; Infiltrator; Ivan "Ironman" Stewart's Super Off-Road; Jordan vs. Bird: One on One; The Magic of Scheherazade; Monster Truck; Nobunaga's Ambition; Ring Raiders; River City Ransom; Rock 'n' Ball; Romance of the Three Kingdoms; Tetris; Tune-up Rallye; Twin Cobra; Urban Convoy; Web World; Xybots, and 720°.

Volume 2

In Volume 2, you'll find reviews of games including: Abadox: The Deadly Inner War; A Boy and His Blob; Adventures of Bayou Billy; Amagon; Astyanax; Back to the Future; Battle of Olympus; Casino Kid; Chessmaster; Faxanadu; Dr. Chaos; Dragon Warrior; DuckTales; HydLide; Iron Tank; King's Knight; Monster Party; Ninja Gaiden; Paperboy; Rollerball; Romance of the Three Kingdoms; Sesame Street ABC; Stealth ATF; Super Sprint; Teenage Mutant Ninja Turtles; Vegas Dream, and Willow.

Also, exciting new sports games including: Bases Loaded II; Baseball Simulator 1.000; Baseball Stars; Dusty Diamond's All-Star Softball; Evert & Lendl Top Players' Tennis; Super Dodge Ball.

And, challenging game shows such as: Anticipation; Hollywood Squares; Jeopardy; Jeopardy Jr.; Wheel of Fortune; Wheel of Fortune Jr.

You'll also read about Golden Oldies including: Athletic World; Bandai Golf: Challenge Pebble Beach; Bomberman; BurgerTime; Ghostbusters; Indiana Jones and the Temple of Doom; RoboWarrior; Lee Trevino's Fighting Golf; PacMan; Seicross; Shooting Range; MagMax, and Taboo: The Sixth Sense.

Acknowledgments

This book bears two names on the cover, but it is the work of dozens of good people, and we wish to extend our thanks.

About the writing: Corey Sandler of Holliston and Nantucket, Massachusetts wore his fingers to the bone on the Game Boy and the keyboard of his computer. His partner, Tom Badgett of Corryton, Tennessee kept the office running and helped on the technical side.

Tom Christopher, a New York artist as apt with a mouse as an oil brush, created the electronic game icons. Marshal M. Rosenthal, also from New York, put his electronic photo studio at our disposal to capture most of the screen pictures for the book.

Our thanks go to the game counselors at many of the Nintendo licensees who spent time with us on the phone sharing some of their best secrets.

Thanks to Kenzi Sugihara, Michael Roney, Terry Nasta, and the other professionals at Bantam Books, and Bill Gladstone and Tracy Smith of Waterside Productions, for getting *Ultimate Unauthorized Nintendo Game Boy Strategies* into print.

We thank again our crew of Nintendo kids, including Rich and Christopher Ehrmann of Holliston, and William and Tessa Sandler of Holliston and Nantucket, Massachusetts.

And grateful thanks to our families for putting up with the strange demands of the writer, especially as deadline time approaches.

This book was put together with the assistance of a number of companies who provided hardware, software, and advice. We'd like to thank the makers of the following computer products and commend them to your attention:

Austin 286/16. An 80286-based personal computer with built-in VGA graphics support, 4 Mbytes of RAM, and a 40-Mbyte hard disk. Austin

Computer Systems, 10300 Metric Blvd., Austin, TX 78758. (800) 752-1577.

CompuAdd 386/20. A 20-MHz 80386 PC with 0 wait state, cache memory. CompuAdd Corporation, 12303 Technology Blvd., Austin, TX 78727. (800) 627-1967.

Fujitsu RX7100-PS Postscript LED printer. Fujitsu America, Inc., 3005 Orchard Drive, San Jose, CA 95134. (408) 423-1300.

NEC Silentwriter LC-890 PostScript LED printer. NEC Information Systems, Inc., 1414 Massachusetts Avenue, Boxboro, MA 01719.

Hijaak and InSet software for image capture and conversion. Inset Systems, 71 Commerce Drive, Brookfield, CT 06804.

Marshal M. Rosenthal Photography. (212) 807-1247.

Contents

·|·
41 Great Game Boy Challenges

·1·
Great Adventures

Batman
AGE: 6 years to Adult
DIFFICULTY: Apprentice-Hot Dog

The Masked Avenger receives his instructions.

Happy Birthday Gotham City! All over town, preparations are underway for the 200th Anniversary of Gotham City Festival. But it's a hollow celebration, for Gotham is in the grip of crime and violence. Suddenly, the entire city is assaulted by deadly DDID Nerve Gas unleashed by Joker, the city's evil leader.

On the side of the good guys is Vicki Vale, a journalist who is tracking the gas. But Vicki is found by the forces of evil and kidnapped.

3

"Then from nowhere appeared a man with a mysterious black shadow." Who could it be? Get serious: It's Batman, of course. The Batman of the dark movie of the same name, a man who lost his parents to crime in his childhood and has since dedicated his life to fighting evil.

This game captures very nicely the dark feeling of the hit motion picture; our sources at Sunsoft tell us that the stars of that movie insisted on creative control over the Nintendo games that grew out of the film. You know this cartridge has a little extra right from the start, as you watch a Batman logo spin into sight like a tumbling pizza. The designers seem to have extracted every bit of possible detail from the limited Game Boy screen for the opening comic book-like scenes.

There's an eerie opening musical selection that sounds like an electronic synthesizer later changing over to a guitar and drum sound.

For the record, we are told that Batman does not use guns. He uses weapons. Weapons that shoot. Whatever.

We worked from a prototype of the game.

With this Game Boy release, we note yet another multimedia escapade for the Masked Avenger. He started out in pulp comic books, of course, and still resides there. But Batman has branched out into bubble gum cards, a television series, a major motion picture, PC games and Nintendo games, each different.

The Story of Batman

Batman was born more than 50 years ago, out of the dark and threatening days that led up to World War II, when it seemed that all of the world was about to explode into violence and hatred. We spoke to the keepers of the flame at DC Comics for a bit of background.

In May of 1939, artist Bob Kane and writer Bill Finger created for Detective Comics a character who was determined to stand up all by himself against the forces of evil. He had seen his parents gunned down by a stick-up man, and had sworn to dedicate his life to law and order . . . and revenge. Thus he started his "professional" life as a possessed killer.

In an early edition of Detective Comics that recounted the birth of the caped avenger, Bruce Wayne sees a sinister flying creature outside his window in Gotham City and speaks these words:

"Criminals are a superstitious, cowardly lot. My disguise must be able to strike terror into their hearts. I must become a creature of the night—dark, terrible . . . A BAT! That's IT! It's an OMEN! I shall become a BAT!"

In the early Batman stories, the avenger acted alone. But in April of 1940, Batman picked up a sidekick, Robin, who gave a softer character to the ongoing story, but did not soften the vengeful Batman himself. Robin has moved in and out of the Batman story over the years.

Later in 1940, Batman got his own comic book, and in Batman #1, two arch-enemies were introduced: The Joker and Catwoman. The Penguin and The Riddler came later. Through the war and into the 1950s, the stories continued in their dark and moody vein. Later in the '50s, the story lines began to become more fanciful, and a number of "relatives" were added to the cast, including Batwoman, Bat-Mite and Bat-Hound. There were stories that brought in alien creatures and science fiction themes. These themes continued until 1964, when the writers of the comic books turned back to the rougher and more realistic stories of the original Batman.

Throughout his history, Batman has been a multimedia guy. His first movie appearance was in 1943 in a Columbia Pictures movie serial called "Batman." A second serial called "Batman and Robin" was launched in 1948. The first newspaper comic strip began in 1943, and was revived in 1966. His first electronic appearance was as a guest star on the "Superman" radio show in the 1940s.

Batman became a television superstar in 1966 with the launch of the "Batman" TV series. The show, which ran for three seasons, was very different from the original Batman themes. The show was silly and frivolous and a lot of fun. The tone of the comic books again changed, reflecting the high "camp" of the TV show.

In the 1970s, the Batman comics returned to the darker themes of the original Batman. Today, Batman is published in almost every comic book format, in more than 20 languages in 45 countries around the world.

Batman celebrated his 50th birthday with the release of his first full movie, "Batman," starring Michael Keaton as the Dark Knight and Jack Nicholson as The Joker. And part of the tidal wave of new Batman products that came out along with the movie were the Batman PC game. The caped crusader arrived on the Nintendo Entertainment System and the Nintendo Game Boy in 1990.

MANUFACTURER: Sun Electronics Corp. / (312) 350-8800

NUMBER OF PLAYERS: 1

CHARACTERS

You are the Caped Crusader, the Masked Avenger, that batty Batman, in search of the evil Joker who has kidnapped the fair maiden Vicki Vale.

CONTROL PAD

Arrows: In the Action-Play stages, move Batman left or right. Push down to make Batman crouch. In the Shooting-Play stages, controls the movements of the Batwing up, down or sideways.

"A" BUTTON: In the Action-Play stages, makes Batman jump. The longer the button is held down, the higher he will jump. Note that Batman can move to the left or right while jumping, an important ability when he flies over obstacles or gaps between buildings. In Shooting-Play stages, fires missiles in the forward direction; hold down the button for continuous fire.

"B" BUTTON: In the early Action-Play stages, fires one of Batman's weapons. Note that some weapons are more powerful than others, and further that some enemies are tougher to knock down than others. In Shooting-Play stages, fires missiles backwards; hold down the button for continuous fire.

PAUSE

Press Start to pause the game; press the button again to resume play. See also Timing.

NUMBER OF WORLDS

STAGE 1 (Action Stage)
  Area 1: Gotham City
  Area 2: AXIS Chemical Factory
STAGE 2 (Action Stage)
  Area 1: Gotham City
  Areas 2 and 3: Flugelheim Museum
STAGE 3 (Shooting Stage)
  Areas 1 and 2: Air Fighting above Gotham City
STAGE 4 (Action Stage)
  Areas 1 and 2*: Gotham City Cathedral.
The Boss

* Note that Stage 4-2 is a "forced-scroll area" where Batman's movements from left to right are not under the control of the player. There is no way to escape the ultimate confrontation with the Joker, except by losing.

NUMBER OF LIVES

Batman starts the game with four lives. He'll lose one when the Life Gauge reaches zero, or if he falls down a canyon or gap between buildings.

The battle is underway.

TIMING

The game is not timed, and although the Start button can be used to pause the game, you can also merely stop moving Batman (assuming he is not being attacked) and not lose any points while you take a break.

SCORING POINTS

Batman will earn points for each of the bad guys he dispatches, starting with 50 points per evildoer in early rounds. In addition, he will earn 10 points for each brick he shatters with a projectile from his weapon.

You will earn an additional life at 100,000 points, 200,000 points, 300,000 points, 400,000 points, 500,000 points, 700,000 points and 1,000,000 points. After that it will cost a cool million points for each additional Caped Crusader.

SPECIAL ITEMS

Batman will find a number of special items hidden about in Gotham City. As you move through the world, look for hollow and solid bricks scattered around. The hollow (the manual calls them white, although there is no such color on the Game Boy) are empty. The solid (called black in the manual) contain goodies that will be exposed when they are shot. Batman must jump up and touch the exposed item to capture them.

By the way, we call them goodies, but one of them is a baddie. Try to avoid grabbing it.

The items include:

Weapon Up. Accelerates the firing effectiveness of Batman's current weapon, through level 7 only. Note that the tranquilizer gun can— oops, we mean tranquilizer weapon—not be improved.

Weapon Down. Decelerates the firing effectiveness of the current weapon.

Shield. This special item will whirl around Batman's body and protect him from enemy shots, although the shield will disappear once it has been damaged. There is also a Fast Shield that whirls even faster.

WEAPON ITEMS

Normal. A circled N is the symbol for Batman's starting weapon. Its range is across the full screen, but projectiles will not go through walls or other obstacles.

Shot. This weapon's firing range is shorter than the normal weapon, but capable of continuous firing.

Power. This weapon will send its projectiles through walls.

Wave. This weapon sends out waves of power that can extend across the full screen and through wall-like obstacles.

Batarang. This device shoots out Batman's special boomerangs, which can penetrate walls.

Tranquilizer. The most powerful of Batman's weapons, it will easily shoot through walls. It cannot be fired continuously.

Smoke Bullet. This item will blanket all enemies shown on the screen, clearing them away.

BONUS ITEMS

Bonus. Look for the circled B to earn 5,000 bonus points.

Heart. Worth one point on the Life Gauge.

Batman. Worth an extra life.

POWER PLAYER HINTS

You don't have to stop and fight every bad guy you meet; some you can just jump right over. And be sure to take advantage of Batman's ability to fire his weapon when he is in a crouch or in mid-leap. There are many situations where Batman can shoot over the top of a brick or block while staying out of the line of fire or from mid-air.

CONTINUING

After you lose all of your lives, you will be offered a choice to Continue or End your play. In the early parts of the game (Stage 1 Areas 1 and 2) the Continue brings you right back to the start, which is no improvement over starting over again. In Stage 1 Area 3 or the Boss Area, you will continue from the beginning of Area 3. In the later parts of the game, you will continue from the first area of the current stage.

RESETTING

To reset the game and return to the title screen, press the Start, A, B and Select buttons at the same time.

Batman is a trademark of DC Comics, Inc. © 1989 DC Comics, Inc. Game pak © 1990 Sunsoft.

Castlevania—The Adventure
AGE: 6 years to Adult
DIFFICULTY: Apprentice-Master of the Game

Drac's back, and he's in your pocket. Somehow the evil Count Dracula has managed to survive the harrowing adventures of Castlevania and Simon's Quest on the NES system.

"Desiring revenge even more than blood, he'll descend upon your Game Boy with fangs glistening by the light of the silvery full moon," say the designers at Konami. Yipes!

The old Count Drac packs a great deal of detail and play action into the tiny Game Boy cartridge. You'll go across fields in the traditional left to right scroll. You'll go up and down ladders, stairs and vines. You'll move back from right to left across mountain valleys and then jump over rolling boulders that try to knock you off bridges.

It's a world of mazes and torture chambers and vampire crypts. Your goal is to unlock the secrets of the castle, using special items including hearts, crystals and crosses. You are armed with the Mystic Whip and a great deal of (foolish?) courage.

The Game Boy cartridge is the third in a series (thus far) of four Castlevania games. The first offering, for the NES, was Castlevania, which was a groundbreaking action game with whips and monsters and pits and all that good stuff. The first sequel was Castlevania II: Simon's Quest,

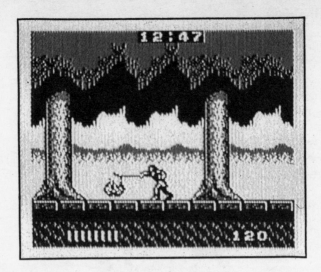

Using the whip.

which was more of an adventure game. In that game, Simon must collect his scattered body parts and then return to the castle for one last battle against the Count. The quest travels through graveyards, castles, forests, lakes and villages. Weapons include five different kinds of whips and numerous magic potions.

MANUFACTURER: Konami / (708) 215-5111

NUMBER OF PLAYERS: 1

CHARACTERS: It's you. And Count Dracula.

CONTROL PAD

Arrows: Press Left or Right to move in those directions. Press Up to climb a rope or stairs. Press Down to descend a rope or stairs, or to duck under the attack of an enemy.

"A" BUTTON: Press the **A button** to leap, or to jump down from a rope.

"B" BUTTON: Press the **B button** to attack with the Mystic Whip in the direction you are currently facing.

Jump over the bouncing eyeballs.

PAUSE

Press the Start button to pause the game; press the button again to resume play.

NUMBER OF WORLDS

There are four levels of dungeons, torture chambers and crypts. At the end of each of the first three levels you will meet up with a Primary Evil you will have to defeat before you can advance to the next level.

At the end of the fourth level, you will enter the "dead" of night and come neck to neck with the Count (we're not talking about Sesame Street here) himself. You must defeat Dracula or be drafted into his army of vampires forever, or at least until you turn off the power switch.

NUMBER OF LIVES

You start the game with four lives. You can gain an extra life at 10,000 points, and for every 20,000 points after then.

TIMING

Each stage has a time limit, displayed at the top center of the screen. (The first round grants you 13 minutes and 15 seconds of screen time: by our calculations, the game's clock ran about 20 percent faster than real time, meaning you probably have just over 10 minutes to complete the opening

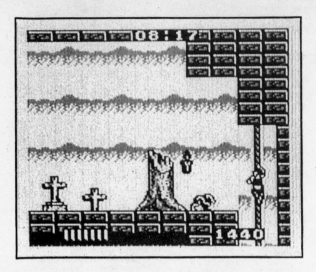

Keep climbing when you reach the first tree stumps . . .

level.) If time runs out in a particular level before you have defeated Count Dracula or the Primary Evil, you will lose the game.

SCREEN DISPLAY

At the top center of the screen you will see the remaining time for the level you are in. At the bottom left is the indicator of your remaining life strength. You start the game with 10 ticks on the meter, and will lose one each time you are hit. At the bottom right is the current score.

When you enter into the "One on One" battle with one of the Primary Evils or the Count himself, the score display will be replaced by a meter of the remaining life force for your evil opponent.

SECRET WEAPONS

Key to the success of your quest in the castle will be your capture and use of various special items. Most of the items can be obtained by lighting the wicks of the candles you see scattered about in the castle; do this by approaching them and flicking your whip at the wick. (Flick my wick?)

The items are:

Hearts. They will partially restore your Life Line.
Flashing Hearts. Will completely restore your Life Line.
1 Up. Gives you an extra life, which may—or may not—be enough.

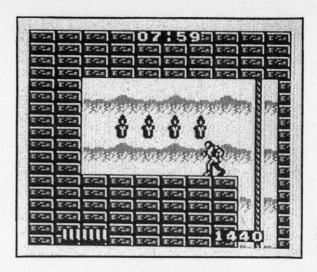

... to reach the first secret room.

Cross of Gold. Makes you invincible for a short period of time. Grab every one you can; they are especially helpful as protection while you are climbing ropes,

Crystal. Increases the power of your Mystic Whip. The first crystal will make your crystal longer and stronger. The second crystal you obtain will allow you to shoot fireballs. Later crystals do not affect the power of your whip.

Coin. Increases your point total.

Flashing Crystal. Calls forth one of the Primary Evils for the final battle of each level.

ENEMIES

Well, you know about the Count, right? He's bad, but so are his guardians. First there are the various attackers you will meet as you scoot along. They include:

Big Eye. Which is exactly what it looks like. They'll come rolling along at you at the most difficult moments. Jump over them if you can, or crouch down and use your whip: aim carefully, for you will probably get only one chance.

Madman. A hero only to his mummy.

Punaguchi. A fist with teeth, or is it a nasty mouth with knuckles?

Death Bat. A scooting skeleton.

Evil Armor. Have you ever had a knight like this?

The She Worm. One of the most difficult to get by, a real slug of a gal.

And then there are the three Primary Evils:

Gobanz. He carries a mace and waits for you at the end of Level 1.

Under Mole.

Zeldo.

I ALWAYS WANTED TO KNOW

Where in the World are these promised 1-Ups? I could use an extra life or two. There are not that many scattered about. You'll find one in the secret room on the first level (What secret room? Read Super Secret, next) and you'll find one just after the sixth ladder. As with the other special items, you need to light the candles with your whip and then grab the booty that drops to earth.

SUPER SECRET!

Hidden in each level of the game are secret rooms just packed with those weapons and special items and 1-Ups you would love to have but are too shy to ask the Count to borrow. (Yeah, right.)

In Level 1, keep track of the number of ropes you have climbed. Wait for number 5. (You'll know you're at the right place when you see tree stumps instead of full trees.) Don't get off the fifth rope; instead keep climbing up, up and up. Yes, we do want you to go right through those bricks. They're not really there. When you get to the top, you'll be in a small chamber with four candles that will give you extra life, strength and power. Don't leave without them all. After you've grabbed the goodies, climb back down the rope and continue your quest.

In Level 3, climb the rope and then jump off to the right after you have escaped the spikes. In Level 4, the room is available by walking across an invisible platform: keep searching, you'll find it.

DANGER!

You cannot attack with the Mystic Whip while you are climbing up or down a rope.

Watch out for hidden traps on each level. You probably will fall into each of them a few times—places like the Pit of Pit Vipers—but remember that they will always be in the same place in each game, so you will eventually begin to know where they are.

POWER PLAYER HINTS

Learn to zap your whip in mid-jump. It is a good maneuver for combat and it is the only way to light some of the candles that you will find suspended in mid-air. Remember, too, not to get too close to a candle or an enemy before you flick your whip. The damage is done by the end of the whip, and the whip needs to be fully extended to do its work.

CONTINUING

You can continue to try to defeat the Count as many times as you dare. All you have to do is use the arrow keys to move the cursor to select YES on the Continue screen at the end of the game and then press the **A button.** You will continue your quest from the start of the level where you most recently died.

Castlevania—The Adventure is a trademark of Konami Inc. Konami is a registered trademark of Konami Industry Co., Ltd. © 1989 Konami Inc.

Fist of the North Star

AGE: 6 years-Adult
DIFFICULTY: Apprentice

A nuclear war has devastated the planet. Why a war? Between which enemies? How did they come to use nuclear weapons? We don't know.

But anyhow, the leaders of the remaining power groups are continuing their quests for supremacy amongst the ruins. There are, as there always seem to be, both good guys and bad guys.

More to the point is the title screen that says: "Ten Big Brawls for King of the Universe." That's more like it.

Among the forces of good is Kenshiro, the legendary Fist of the North Star. (His friends call him Ken.) His goal is to defeat the bad guys and rebuild a peaceful new society. But then there are those who have their own ideas, including an evil brother and even a not-so-evil brother who doesn't know he's a brother.

It's a round-robin battle to the end, with the new world hanging in the balance. And guess what: you can choose to play the good guy, or you can take the side of the bad folk.

Each of the characters has a different set of abilities. Some are physical powerhouses, while others have learned to concentrate their strength into

Looks like a mismatch to us.

mental energy with such strange tools as the Aura Wave and the Vacuum Drain.

The basic game (called the Normal Mode) pits you against each of the other characters. In the VS Mode, two players compete in head-to-head action using a single character they have selected. And finally, there is a Team Mode, in which two players each select a team of five characters and then launch into a round-robin fight to the death; the last character still standing at the end wins the game.

This is the second version of Fist of the North Star for Nintendo gamesters. A pak for the NES is offered by Taxan. In that game our hero Ken has to fight through eight scenes, using his bare fist, guns, bombs and most of all, the mysterious art of Gento Karate to rescue the people of the Central Imperial Capital, held captive by the evil Emperor Heaven.

We worked with an early prototype of the Game Boy pak.

MANUFACTURER: Electro Brain / (801) 531-0324

NUMBER OF PLAYERS: 1 or 2.

CONTROL PAD

The actions of the various characters—good or bad—differ slightly, depending upon the nature of their special abilities. All of the characters have a special ability assigned to the **A Button**; only some of them also can launch an attack using the **B Button**. Read the descriptions of each under the Character section below.

Arrows: The Left or Right arrow moves your character in those directions. The Up arrow makes the character jump, while the Down arrow makes him kneel. Use the arrows in combination with the **A or B Button** for special attacks.

Note that musclebound Heart and Uygur cannot kneel or jump and can only crash head-on into their enemies,

CHARACTERS

To examine the current status of each character before a match begins, call up the Parameter Display screen by holding down the Select button and pressing the **A Button** before you choose a type of game to play. Once you are into the Parameter Display, you can cycle between the various characters by using the Up or Down arrows.

Kenshiro. The legendary heir to the Hokuto Shinken, the 2,000-year-old martial arts academy. He puts his prodigious powers to play for the people, for whom he is regarded as a great protector. The bad guys, naturally, regard him as an unpleasant dude. He has seven scars on his chest, said to resemble in shape the constellation of the North Stars.

Kenshiro's special tactics are:
A Button: Punch or Aura Wave
B Button: Kick

Here are Kenshiro's starting parameters:

Kenshiro.
Level	1
Experience	0
Attack A	20
Attack B	50
Defense	20

Heart. An awesome, ugly giant whose skin is so tough and leathery it acts like armor plating; almost nothing can stop him when he uses his body to crash into an enemy. Heart is so big, though, that he cannot kneel or jump.

A Button: Punch
B Button: Body Crash

Here are Heart's starting parameters:

Heart.
Level	1
Experience	0
Attack A	16
Attack B	30
Defense	25

Shin. Oh yeah, Kenshiro? Think the Hokuto Shinken is so tough? This guy Shin is the heir to the Nanto Shinken, a rival martial arts academy. According to some reports, this guy possesses a power called the Vacuum Drain, that can destroy enemies at great distances.

A Button: Punch or Vacuum Drain
B Button: No power

Here are Shin's starting parameters:

Shin.
Level	1
Experience	0
Attack A	35
Attack B	0
Defense	16

Jagi. This distant relative by marriage is not quite as good as Kenshiro, but he's a whole lot more angry, and he has mastered a nefarious needle attack. The anger comes from the fact that he was passed over for official designation as heir of the Hokuto Shinken. You don't suppose he would try to take on Kenshiro, do you?

A Button: Punch and Needle Attack
B Button: No power

Here are Jagi's starting parameters:

Jagi.
Level	1
Experience	0
Attack A	20
Attack B	0
Defense	16

Uygur. Oh you big brute you Uygur. The guardian of the frightening town of Kasandra, he is even bigger than heart, and a whole lot more

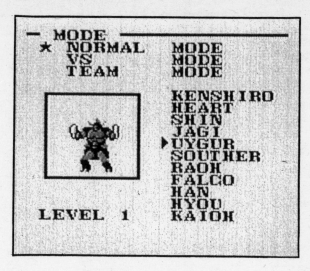

The player selection screen.

agile. He can use a whip with the best of them, but he also can produce a body crash called the Mongolian Destruction that you've got to see to believe. Better to see it than to feel it. Like Heart, Uygur is just too big a boy to kneel or jump.

A Button: Whip
B Button: Mongolian Destruction Body Crash

Here are Uygur's starting parameters:

Uygur.

Level	1
Experience	0
Attack A	21
Attack B	35
Defense	30

Souther. Also known as the Southern Emperor, he is another pretender to the throne, this time to the Nanto Shinken school. Like his cousin Shin, he also can use the Vacuum Drain; his powers are even stronger at close range, but less so from further away.

A Button: Punch or Vacuum Drain
B Button: No power

Here are Souther's starting parameters:

Souther.

Level	1
Experience	0
Attack A	40
Attack B	0
Defense	28

Raoh. Ow! He is the oldest brother-in-law to Kenshiro, and possesses skills from both of the rival skills, Nanto and Hokuto. He is said to fear no one and no thing, relying on his awesome Aura Wave.

A Button: Punch or Aura Wave
B Button: Kick

Here are Raoh's starting parameters:

Raoh.

Level	1
Experience	0
Attack A	26
Attack B	60
Defense	38

Falco. He is one of the heirs to yet another school, the Gento Kouken, and is well known for his mastery of mental energy attacks. His Aura Wave is said to be not quite as powerful as Raoh's, but it is more concentrated and if it hits something is more likely to make an impact than Raoh's is.

A Button: Punch or Aura Wave
B Button: Kick

Here are Falco's starting parameters:

Falco.

Level	1
Experience	0
Attack A	24
Attack B	55
Defense	35

Han. Are you keeping all of these heirs and Hokutos straight? Why? Anyhow, this guy Han is an heir to the Hokuto Ryuken. More important, he is ranked third in the line of power in the kingdom of Shura.

A consummate fighter, he possesses a neat Aura Wave attack, but he is best known for his super-fast (so quick they're invisible) fists.

A Button: Punch or Aura Wave
B Button: Kick

Here are Han's starting parameters:

Han.
Level	1
Experience	0
Attack A	26
Attack B	58
Defense	40

Hyou. Move over, Han. Hyou is the second most powerful guy in the kingdom of Shura, and also an heir to Hokuto Ryuken. But wait: Hyou and Kenshiro are actually brothers, although Hyou doesn't know this since the evil Kaioh used an ancient mental technique to erase all such memories from Hyou's mind. And thus Hyou is fighting his brother!

A Button: Punch or Aura Wave
B Button: Kick

Here are Hyou's starting parameters:

Hyou.
Level	1
Experience	0
Attack A	28
Attack B	65
Defense	40

Kaioh. But wait! Here's the Supreme Commander of the kingdom of Shura, himself. And also an heir to Hokuto Ryuken, of course. Like Kenshiro and Hyou, he's a master of martial arts, but unlike those other guys, he uses his powers for evil purposes—he is so bad that some call him Kaioh the Devil. What is even more evil is that Kaioh is also a brother to Kenshiro—and poor confused Hyou, of course. He fights against Kenshiro and others using a range of weapons including an especially powerful mental attack called the Matoki.

A Button: Punch or Matoki Aura Wave
B Button: Kick

Here are Kaioh's starting parameters:

Kaioh.

Level	1
Experience	0
Attack A	28
Attack B	70
Defense	40

PAUSE

Press the Start button to pause the game; press the button again to resume play.

ENERGY LEVELS

In the Normal Mode, your energy level will be completely restored when you finish a stage—one way or another. If you win and move on to the next stage, you will start rested and recharged; if you lose and the game is over, you will start a replay of the same battle (using the Continue option) with full energy.

In VS Mode, play is over when one player defeats the other. What happens if the fight ends in a draw? Both players lose.

The unusual Team Mode for this game allows each player to choose 5 characters for his team. Each time one or the other of the players loses a character, the battle will continue with a replacement. The challenge will go on until one or the other player has lost all of his characters.

SCREEN DISPLAY

At the upper left corner of the screen is the Energy Meter for player 1. The enemy's meter is shown at the upper right corner. Each player's Attack Power Meter will be displayed below the energy meter when a battle is underway.

USING PASSWORDS

Fist of the North Star offers continues any time you do lose a life.

At the end of any round in which you lose, the game will offer a password. Write down the password and use it to re-enter the game at a later time. We'd advise you display and record the password every time it is offered so that you can continue to work your way through the game without having to refight old battles.

The passwords are fairly complex combinations of 14 letters and numbers. Be sure to write them down carefully and enter them into the game exactly as you have written them. Be sure to note the difference between 0s (displayed with a slash through the character) and Os, and 1s and ls.

Here's a sample password that super-champ Willie received about halfway through a complete competition:

XKP   72QN
VHR   JGU5

Gargoyle's Quest

AGE: 7 years to Adult
DIFFICULTY: Apprentice-Master of the Game

This is an unusual mix of adventure and role playing, squeezed tightly into the tiny Game Boy package.

You are Firebrand, guardian Gargoyle of the friendly Ghoul Realm. According to Legend, many many years ago, the Ghoul Realm had been invaded by an alien force known only as the Destroyers. The bad guys had almost succeeded in capturing the land, when suddenly a mysterious, powerful fire descended from the sky and destroyed the Destroyers.

The secret of that fire, alas, has been lost. And guess what: the Destroyers are back!

The only clue is this: according to the legend, the sole heir to the Red Gargoyle can bring back the magic flame. As Firebrand, you set out to discover the heir to the avenging flame and bring peace to the kingdom once again.

There are two windows into this game. The first view you have is from above. You'll look down on Firebrand as he moves above, searching for clues and information in inside and outside scenes. There is no combat in this mode.

The second vantage point is from the side. You'll look on from alongside Firebrand in all of the battles. When you complete a search or a battle, you'll return to the overhead view.

As you travel through the Above-view areas, you may find the entrances to several secret combat zones. If you end up within one, you will have to defeat the enemies in order to get back out. But wait! When you first meet a creature, spend the time to get to know him: Talk to him first before you start fighting, and you may find he or it is a friend with secret information for you.

Gargoyle's Quest is a world of fantastic scenery, with lots of volcanoes, wicked forest creatures and other amazing sights. And we mustn't overlook Gargoyle himself, a small guy with bat-like wings and claws on his hands and feet.

MANUFACTURER: Capcom / (408) 727-1665

NUMBER OF PLAYERS: 1.

CHARACTERS: You are Firebrand.

CONTROL PAD
The controls will work differently, depending on whether you are in the Above or Side view.

ABOVE VIEW
Arrows: Move Firebrand Up, Down, Left or Right.

> **"A" BUTTON:** In most areas, pressing the **A Button** will bring up a special menu on the screen. The menu has four choices:
>
> > **TALK.** Instructs Firebrand to talk to any characters he is facing. To continue the dialogue, press the A Button.
> >
> > **USE.** Tells Firebrand to use one of the Magic items in his possession.
> >
> > **LVL.** Asks the computer to display the current status of Firebrand (including Level) and the items he possesses.
> >
> > **CHK.** Asks the computer to Check (Examine or Obtain) any items found.
>
> Press the **A Button** together with the Up arrow to move Firebrand up a vertical wall.
>
> **"B" BUTTON:** Cancels any screen, returning you to the Above View mode.

SIDE VIEW
Arrows: The Left and Right arrows move Firebrand in those directions. The Up and Down arrows do not function in this mode.

> **"A" BUTTON:** Press this button to begin the process of flight. Pressing the **A Button** once will make Firebrand jump or fly for a short period of time. Press the **A Button** a second time while

Firebrand is in the air will extend his flying time. If you press the
A Button a third time, you will bring him down to earth quicker.

"B" BUTTON: Press the **B Button** makes Firebrand use his weapon.
He starts the game with a fiery missile; some enemies will require
more than one hit before they will bite the dust.

START: Press the Start button during play to display the current game
statistics. The stats are:

L. Life Force. Each character begins the game with two life forces.

W. Wing Force. Displays how much available energy Firebrand has
for flying.

J. Jumping Power. Yes, you're right: available jumping power.

VIALS. The number of vials of magic Firebrand has picked up, and
are available to purchase items.

ICONS. The number of characters available to the player.

PAUSE

You can use the Start to pause the game since it will display on screen
the current game statistics; press Start again to resume play.

NUMBER OF LIVES 3.

I ALWAYS WANTED TO KNOW

What exactly is a Gargoyle, anyway? Would you believe a drain spout?

Gargoyles are the grotesque carved stone figures often found on
Gothic buildings at the roof or eaves. Originally the term meant the
unadorned spout that extended outward from a rain gutter or parapet; the
gargoyle allowed water to fall free of the building, preventing seepage
and damage to masonry.

Medieval carvers became a bit playful and gave the spout a carved
head or body with grotesque features. Superstition held that the gargoyle
frightened away evil spirits while serving its practical function. By the
16th century, the lead drain pipe had been invented, but the gargoyles
were retained for some time afterwards, because they were so darned
pretty.

SUPER SECRET!

Our inside sources tell us the whole key is to learn to fly.

POWER PLAYER HINTS

Use Firebrand's powerful claws to attach yourself to walls and other surfaces. While you're hanging around, you can still use your firebreathing weapon, flaming out in the direction away from the wall.

Use the **A Button** and the Up Arrow to move Firebrand up a wall. Use the **A Button** to move him up the wall a bit to avoid hazards when necessary.

The real key to success in this game is to master the art of flying. Practice makes almost perfect.

USING PASSWORDS

The game will give you a password allowing reentry into the deep reaches of the game.

Gargoyle's Quest is a trademark of Capcom USA. © Capcom USA.

Gauntlet II

AGE: 6 years-Adult
DIFFICULTY:Apprentice-Hot Dog

The fearsome foursome are back: Thor, Thyra, Questor and Merlin, come thundering right into the palm of your hand, in Gauntlet II. The original Gauntlet was a big hit in the arcades and in a Nintendo Entertainment System version from Tengen.

Just when you thought you had explored every corner of the terrible Dark Dungeons, along come our great warriors. You'll be on the hunt for your basic special treasures, potions and amulets; you've got to look out for traps, poisoned food, force fields and assorted ghoulies.

We looked at the IBM PC version of Gauntlet II, also from Mindscape. The NES and Game Boy versions were planned to be similar, but not all villains will be included. The Game Boy version will include a few extra features, such as two-player explorations using the Video Link cable, and digitized voices and sound effects.

MANUFACTURER: Mindscape / (708) 480-8715

NUMBER OF PLAYERS

1 or 2. The two-player games requires two copies of the game cartridge, a pair of Game Boys and a Video Link cable.

CHARACTERS
THOR the Warrior
Armor: This guy is so tough that his skin alone blocks about 20 percent of damage.

Shot Power: Twice normal.

Hand to Hand Battling: An excellent warrior with the Battle Axe, he can destroy monster generators.

Magic Power: Not his strong point, he can damage some monsters but no generators.

THYRA the Valkyrie
Armor: She carries a shield that can eliminate about 30 percent of damage.

Shot Power: Not so hot.

Hand to Hand Battling: Pretty good with a Sword, she can destroy monster generators.

Magic Power: Moderate, she can damage most monsters and generators.

MERLIN the Wizard
Armor: None. Zip. Zero.

Shot Power: Good, nothing to write home about.

Hand to Hand Battling: He doesn't even carry a weapon.

Magic Power: Stand back. What else would you expect from a wizard? Merlin can damage all monsters and generators.

QUESTOR the Elf

Armor: Would you believe this guy goes into battle wearing a leather jacket? Eliminates about 10 percent of the damage.

Shot Power: Poor.

Hand to Hand Battling: Moderate, he carries a Dagger. But he cannot destroy monster generators.

Magic Power: Very good, Questor can destroy almost all monsters and generators.

VILLAINS

All around the dungeons are Monster Generators that create particular types of monsters. There are three levels of generators; depending on the power it possesses, the monsters it produces require one, two or three hits to be killed. The Generators themselves can be destroyed, too.

Ghosts. Stay away. They'll hit you only once, doing a lot of damage, and then disappear. Shoot them—don't try to fight hand-to-hand.

Grunts. They'll run right up to you and try to bash you with clubs. Shoot them or fight them in close.

Demons. They'll throw fireballs, or try to bite you if they can get close enough.

Lobbers. These nasties will try to do you in by throwing rocks over the wall at you. They'll run away from you if you get close, and so you must shoot them or trap them in a corner and fight them up close.

Sorcerers and Super Sorcerers. About as hard to pin down as a ghost, these guys will disappear as they move. You cannot shoot them when they are invisible. You can momentarily stun them with magic; shoot them to destroy them.

Death. Death can be hazardous to your health, taking away up to 200 points, and then die himself. Your only defense is to shoot him—don't try to fight him—before he gets too close.

Acid Puddles. These guys can really burn you.

IT. A glowing, spinning disk. When it hits you, you are "it." All monsters will then be attracted to you until you leave the maze or touch another player, who then becomes "it."

Watch out also for **The Thief,** who will try to steal items from the richest player—if he gets away without being shot, he will leave his booty on the next level. And **The Mugger** can rob the richest player of some of his health.

CONTROL PAD

Arrows: Moves the character Up, Down, Left or Right in the maze.
"A" BUTTON: Use for magic potions.
"B" BUTTON: Use for weapons.

SPECIAL ITEMS

Scattered around the dungeons are various important objects. Some of them are worth collecting, and others are definitely worth avoiding. Here are some of them:

Potions. The ordinary, run-of-the-mill potions will give you the power to stun or destroy monsters or the monster generators.

Special Potions. These are, well, special. They offer extra powers, as in:

Extra Armor. The shield increases protection from hits.

Extra Magic Power. This special bottle increases the effect of all potions.

Extra Shot Speed. Look for the lightning bolt to add some speed to your weapons.

Extra Shot Power. The bullseye turbocharges your weapons.

Extra Fight Power. The special sword improves your hand-to-hand fighting ability.

Extra Pick-Up Power. Give yourself a hand, and be able to carry 15 instead of 10 items.

Food or Cider. Increases your health by 100 points.

Keys. And what do we use keys for, class? Each one collected adds 100 points to your score. And, if you do not engage in a fight for about 30 seconds after you grab one, all locked doors will open by themselves.

Treasure. Worth 100 points. Some of them are locked. Not all chests contain good things, though!

Amulets. These magical devices confer some special powers for a short time, including:

Invisibility.

Invulnerability.

Repulsiveness.

Transportability. (Allows you to run right through solid objects.)

10 Super Shots.

Reflective Shots.

Kung-Fu Kid

AGE:5 years to 18
DIFFICULTY:Apprentice-Hot Dog

Approaching the gate.

You can punch and kick all day using just your thumbs when playing Kung-Fu Kid in its new Game Boy incarnation.

Like most martial arts games available for the full-sized Nintendo Entertainment System, this sort of game will be very appealing to those players who like this sort of game, and not very interesting to those who have no interest in kicking and fighting. Is that clear? Think of it this way: If this is what you are looking for, here's a fine example.

We worked with a very early version of the game. Some of the minor details and names of characters will probably have changed by the time the game pak arrives on store shelves. Here's what we learned:

The evil Yohma-Gundan army has invaded a peaceful Chinese territory and taken over a pair of castles. They have magically transformed the two castles into an Ice Castle (Hyoma-jou) and a deadly hot Fiery Castle

(Enma-jou). They've taken up residence in the Fiery Castle and are using it as their headquarters in a bold attempt to take over the rest of the world.

You are Jac, and you have set out to rescue your kidnapped girlfriend Linlin (and, while you are at it, rescue the free world from the nasty invaders.)

Your ultimate enemy is the evil boss Dragon Shogun. You'll be armed with the all-powerful Legendary Sword at the start, picking up other items as you go on. Some, but not all, of the enemies you defeat will reveal a special item once you dispatch them; other special items are hidden behind rocks or obstacles you must break. Our favorite special item is the "G" gun, which is not exactly a martial art technique, but then again we're not really into kicking and punching ourselves.

Your ultimate special martial arts technique is the Phantom Flip, which can be launched in an upward, downward, left or right direction.

Scattered about the world are about 20 different nasty enemies (9 more than in the original game) and about 30 special items (twice the number of the NES version). Special items include Winged Boots for walking on water.

Included in the Game Boy version is a new warp stage feature that allows you to go back to previous stages to collect needed items.

About the Original NES Game

This is the third go-round for the Kung-Fu guys. First came the arcade game hit and then the NES game pak.

The original Kung-Fu Kid game for the full-sized Nintendo Entertainment System presented a pretty detailed story, especially as Kung-Fu stories go. Princess Min-Min has been princess-napped by monsters, along with the 10 treasures of the land. The people plead with young Kung-Fu masters Jacky and Lee to defeat the bad guys and restore happiness to the land. Our boys Jacky and Lee set off on a methodical assault on the monster's castles, moving from maze to maze as new doors open.

MANUFACTURER: Culture Brain USA / (206) 882-2339

NUMBER OF PLAYERS: 1.

CHARACTERS

You are Jac or Jack or Jacky . . . we haven't seen the final version of the game . . . and you are set out on a bold adventure in hopes of freeing your kidnapped girlfriend Linlin, or perhaps her name is Min-Min.

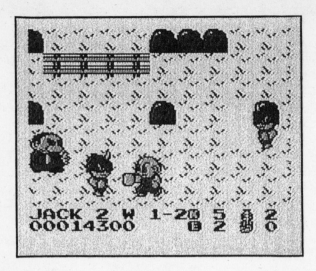

A battle scene.

CONTROL PAD

Arrows: Moves Jac up, down, left or right on the screen. Also used to call up Miracle Kicks when used together with the **B button.**

"A" BUTTON: Throws punches.

"B" BUTTON: Kicks (jump). Press the **B button** together with one of the arrow keys to use one of the Miracle Kicks.

PAUSE

Press the Start button to pause the game; press the Start button again to resume play.

NUMBER OF WORLDS

There are 8 rounds in the game, with 4 stages in each round, for a total of 32 challenges.

The locations are:

1st Round. Fields and gates.
2nd Round. Forests.
3rd Round. Inside the icy cave.
4th Round. Inside the cold castle.
5th Round. The desert.
6th Round. The volcanic belt.
7th Round. Inside the fire cave.
8th Round. The decisive battle inside the Fiery Castle.

In order to move to the next stage, you must defeat 12 enemies at each stage. You will find that there are some enemies that cannot be beaten with ordinary kicks or punches. To get past them you will have to search out, find and use special items which are hidden under blocks and rocks.

NUMBER OF LIVES

You start the game with 5 lives, and will lose one each time you are defeated by an attacker.

TIMING

When you enter the special bonus zone, you will have 20 ticks of the game's clock; the more enemies you defeat in that time, the higher your score.

The rest of the game is not on a timer.

HOW TO CAPTURE THE BEASTIES

Kick and punch. And then kick and punch again. And then you might want to launch a somersaulting Phantom Flip kick and punch.

POWER PLAYER HINTS

Use the Phantom Flip to launch a high-powered assault on your enemies. You can also use the Flip to vault right over some of your oncoming attackers.

When you lose a life, you will return to the game quickly and for a short while your character will be almost transparent. While Jack looks like this, he is invincible; there may be parts of the game where the only way you can get past a particular attacker is to sacrifice one of your lives and then march on by while you are untouchable.

Kung-Fu Kid is a trademark of Culture Brain USA, Inc. © 1990 Culture Brain USA, Inc.

The Amazing Spider-Man

AGE: 6 years-Adult
DIFFICULTY: Apprentice

Our hero.

It's enough to make you climb the wall!

Poor Spider-Man. He's out minding his own business, fighting the forces of evil on behalf of decent folk like you and me, when some no-good useless mutants go and kidnap his wife and threaten to "neutralize" her if their demands are not met.

"This is gonna be a bad day . . ." begins the story of The Amazing Spider-Man in his Game Boy debut. "Here's your chance . . . to guide your favorite web-slinger through some dangerous New York neighborhoods as he goes up against the worst criminal low lifes that the Big Apple can dish out. If that's not enough, at the end of each area is an evil mutant who makes the other criminals seem like they just got out of nursery school."

The Story of Spider-Man

Just who is this person they call Spider-Man anyhow? We posed the question to the folks at Marvel Comics, who chronicle his every adventure each month, and we learned an amazing tale. First of all, the vital statistics:

Real name: Peter Parker
Occupation: Freelance photographer and adventurer
Place of birth: New York City
Height: 5'10"
Weight: 165 pounds
Eyes: Hazel
Hair: Brown
Superhuman powers: He'd be a platinum medalist at the Olympics, able to lift about 10 tons. Beyond that he has the ability to make parts of his body stick to slippery surfaces and possesses an intuitive sense of danger.
Known enemies: Lots of evil guys who like to run around in strange costumes, including the Kingpin, the Vulture, Electro, the Sandman, Mysterio, Dr. Octopus, the Hobgoblin, the Lizard, Jack O'Lantern, the Enforcers, the Scorpion, Silvermane, the Rose, Kraven the Hunter, the Puma, the Rhino, the Tinkerer and the Shocker.

But how did he get that way? Therein lies a story.

Peter Parker was orphaned at the age of six when his parents were killed in an airplane crash, and he was raised by his uncle and aunt, Ben and May Parker, in Forest Hills, N.Y. He was an honor student in science at Midtown High School, where his academic interests overtook his social growth: in other words, he was apparently the school "dweeb."

One night, Peter went to a public demonstration of the safe handling of nuclear laboratory waste materials. Somehow during the demonstration a common house spider (*Achaearanea tepidariorum*) wandered into the path of a particle accelerator's beam and became irradiated. (So much for safe handling of nuclear materials, huh?) The poor spider fell on Peter's hand and gave him a nasty bite.

Peter left the exhibition in pain, and started home through a bad part of the neighborhood. There he was set upon by a gang of hoodlums. Peter, who had never been known as a fighter, reacted with ferocious strength and speed. Then he ran away, right into the path of a speeding oncoming car. At the last moment, he leapt out of the way, and found himself sticking to a wall by his fingertips, 30 feet up in the air. He walked down from the wall along a thin wire.

It took Peter, a bright boy, a few moments to realize that his strange new powers were related to his bite from the radioactive spider.

Peter's first use of his powers was not aimed the most at benefitting the side of good against evil, though. Out on an errand, he sees a poster for a contest in which a professional wrestler is challenging any comer to stay in the ring with him at least three minutes. He puts on a mask (he's shy) and enters the ring where he easily defeats the wrestler. While there, he is spotted by a talent scout who signs him to a television contract for a network variety show.

Peter calls himself the Amazing Spider-Man. He locks himself in the high school laboratory where he builds himself some special equipment for his "act." He concocts a sticky fluid that acts like a spider's silk web, and "spinneret" devices that allow him to spray out the fluid in the shape of a web strand. Oh yes: he also makes himself a nifty costume.

Leaving the television studio, he sees a security guard chasing after a burglar. Acting as Peter the dweeb instead of the Amazing Spider-Man, he steps aside and does not help and the bad guy escapes. A few days later, Peter returns home to find that his Uncle Ben has been murdered; it turns out that the killer was the same burglar Peter had let get by at the television station.

With this awful death, Peter Parker vows to take to the streets as the scourge of evil to avenge his uncle.

Here's what we know about the changes in Peter's system. To begin with, his reflexes have been boosted to about 15 times that of an average human. If he is far enough away, he can react so fast that he can dodge an oncoming bullet.

He can, according to his biographers, "mentally control the flux of inter-atomic attraction between molecular boundary layers." That means he can get sticky, especially in his hands and feet. The Spider-Man also has "Spider Sense" which warns him of potential danger by a tingling sensation at the back of his skull.

His web-shooters, worn on the wrists of his costume, shoot out special web fluid at high pressure. On contact with air the fluid forms an extremely tough, flexible fiber.

His friends call him Spidey.

MANUFACTURER: LJN Toys, Ltd. / (212) 243-6565

CHARACTERS

Our sticky friend Spider-Man is off to save his wife Mary-Jane (he must be really stuck on her.) He'll fight creeps including Mysterio, Hobgoblin, the Scorpion, Rhino, Dr. Octopus and finally, Venom.

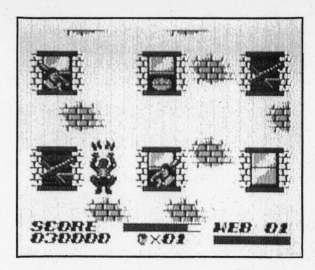

Spider Sense as the Web-Slinger climbs a wall.

CONTROL PAD

The various moves for Spidey are so complex that we're going to present them in two different ways. First, we'll show you the moves that each button will make; then we'll give you an index to all of the moves.

HORIZONTAL SCROLLING AREAS

Arrows: Press Left or Right to walk in those directions. Press Left or Right together with the **A button** for a high jump.
Press Down to Crouch.
Press Down and the **B button** to kick.

"A" BUTTON: Press the **A button** for a small jump.
Press with the Left or Right button for a high jump.

"B" BUTTON: Hold down the **B button** to spin a web.
To swing from a web, do a high jump while holding the **B button**.
Tap the **B button** to throw a punch.
Hold the Down arrow and tap the **B button** to throw a kick.
To throw a flying kick, press the **A button** to jump and then press the **B button.**

WHILE SWINGING FROM A WEB

Arrows: Swing Left or Right using those keys. Press the Down arrow to drop from a web.

"A" BUTTON: Not used.

"B" BUTTON: Hold down the **B button** to spin a web. Tap the **B button** to kick.

IN VERTICALLY SCROLLING AREAS

Arrows:Press the appropriate button to crawl left, right, up or down.

"A" BUTTON:Press Left, Right or Up arrows together with the A button to leap. Release the A button to regain grip.

"B" BUTTON:Press the Left or Right button and tap the B button to kick.

COMMAND INDEX

HORIZONTALLY SCROLLING AREAS

Crouch. Press Down arrow.

Flying Kick. Jump and press the B button.

Kick. Hold the Down arrow and tap the B button.

Large jump. Press the A button together with the left or right arrow key.

Punch. Tap the B button.

Small jump. Press the A button.

Spin web. Hold down the B button.

Swing from a web. Make a large jump and hold the B button.

Walk Left or Right. Press Left or Right arrow.

SWINGING FROM A WEB

Drop from web. Press the Down area.

Kick. Tap the B button.

Spin web. Hold down the B button.

Swing left or right. Press the Left or Right arrow.

VERTICALLY SCROLLING AREAS

Crawl. Press the Left, Right, Up or Down arrow.

Kick. Press the Left or Right arrow and tap the B button.

Leap. Hold the Left, Right or Up arrow and press the A button. Release the A button to regain grip.

NUMBER OF WORLDS

The Alleyway. One of New York's least appreciated tourist attractions. Spidey has to get past hordes of street thugs just to earn the right to battle the evil Mysterio at the end of the level. Jump, punch or use your web spinners to fly through the air. Some of the baddies are carrying things they've stolen from innocent citizens. If you defeat them, they'll drop their booty; grab the stuff to earn points, but don't wait too long or it will disappear. Mysterio waits at the end of the alleyway, hiding behind a cloud of poisonous gas that you must avoid. Your web will have no effect, so use your kicks and punches. Carefully.

A man-to-spider fight.

The Skyscraper. Spidey will have to climb up one of New York's famous skyscrapers, in search of his next opponent, Hobgoblin. Watch out: those people up on the roof are trying to drop things on Spidey's head. And the friendly natives inside the windows have baseball bats that they will swing at the Spider-Man to try to knock him off the wall. If you can launch a kick properly, you'll not only protect yourself but also earn a few points. All the way at the top of the building you'll find one window with an "IN" sign. Jump through it and you're on the roof, where you've got to leap from roof to roof—fighting off more bad guys—before you get what you've been waiting for: a battle against Hobgoblin. Just to make things interesting, he'll come at you from inside his Goblin Glider, through exploding jack-o-lantern bombs at your. Nice guy, huh?

The Subway. The real terror of New York for some people lies underground in the subway. And that's where Spidey heads next, where he must fight against a whole crew of Scorpion's evil team. Spider-Man tries to get past them by running along the top of the subway car, but the bad guys shoot at him and try to trip him from the windows. And, oh yes, there are the deadly subway tunnel bats to watch out for, too. At the end of the tunnel is the Scorpion: watch out for his deadly tail.

Central Park. After the relaxing subway ride, what could be more pleasant than a stroll through New York's famous Central Park? Well, lots of things. Rhino has deployed his troops of evildoers throughout the park, but there is also a whole other world of natural obstacles. Things like killer pigeons and trees that drop exploding seeds. At the end of the park waits Rhino himself, who is quick, strong and dumb.

Downtown. Dr. Octopus is waiting for Spidey at the top of another skyscraper. You're not all that worried about falling flowerpots here. Instead, the bad guys will shoot at you with guns. And, here the buildings are much farther apart and the jumps are more difficult; some of the ledges are not quite as sturdy as they look, either. At the end is the Doc Oc, and he is (ahem) well-armed.

The Sewers. Yes, all of those cute little baby alligators that have been flushed down the toilet really do grow into monsters of the sewer. But down into the muck and crud Spidey must go, in the final challenge of the game. It's safer (and a whole lot cleaner) to stay on the ledges instead of the bottom of the pipe. Watch out for floods. At the end of this pleasant journey you'll find Venom, who has his own very nasty web to use against you.

NUMBER OF LIVES

You start the game with three lives. Each time Spidey is hit or shot, he will lose a bit of his energy; when energy gets low, the energy meter on screen will begin to flash and a beeper will go off to warn you to be careful. When energy is all gone, Spider-Man will lose one of his lives.

SECRET WEAPONS

Spider-Man can shoot his webs to entangle enemies or to give him an instant swinging vine. Use this ability carefully—Spidey has only a limited amount of web fluid and you won't want to run out of the stuff.

SPECIAL ITEMS

Keep an eye out for a hamburger sitting around in one place or another; grab it for a quick-me-up, restoring all of the energy Spidey has lost.

DANGER!Spidey's special weapon, the web, does not work against the nastiest of the nasty, the super boss mutants at the end of each level.

POWER PLAYER HINTS

Spidey Sense, our hero's ability to perceive the presence of danger, will alert you to some events just before they happen. Keep a close watch for little waves floating around his head.

When Spidey is climbing up the skyscraper in the second scene, there is an advanced maneuver that will help him scale the wall quickly: we call it the Great Leap Upward. Combine the Up arrow and the **B button,** being careful to land our hero back on the wall of the building.

CONTINUES

The game includes a limited number of continues that are available after Spider-Man has gone through all of his lives.

·2·
Arcade Games

Alleyway
AGE: 6 to Adult
DIFFICULTY: Apprentice-Master of the Game

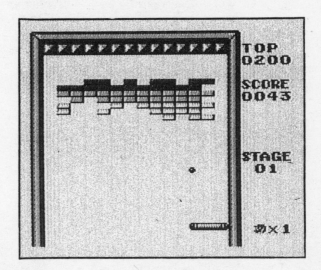

The opening challenge.

Alleyway is a modern Game Boy interpretation of one of the oldest of video games. Why, this game is so old, it was around when Mario and Luigi were in diapers. Similar earlier games bore names including "Breakout" and "Arkanoid."

The goal of this game is to move a paddle left and right across the bottom of the screen to be beneath a falling ball, redirecting it back up to break a

43

row of blocks at the top of the screen. When all of the blocks are destroyed, you will move on to a next, more difficult stage.

Like most good games, it is deceptively simple and increasingly challenging. The first screen, for example, is pretty basic, with a stationary row of blocks at the top. By the second screen, though, the group of blocks at the top starts to move across from right to left. Later on the blocks will start to drop down toward you. And, there are the bonus stages, at least one of which includes a set of blocks in the familiar shape of a short Italian guy with a dopey brother.

After Stage 4, when the ball hits the ceiling the size of your trusty paddle will be reduced.

There is just a touch of music in this game at the end of each level. Instead, the only noises are the bings and beeps the game assigns to the walls, ceilings, blocks and paddles. The result is an appropriate intensity.

By the way, on the box for this game Nintendo describes Alleyway as "Interstellar pingpong with a deadly energy ball!" According to the box, "Your spaceship is at the gate of the Alleyway. Use your vessel to repel the energy ball. Atomize space grids with your return shots." In a world of hype, that description may be worth a blue ribbon prize; there's not a hint of such a space story in this game, but that's all right: it's still a lot of fun and a well-created game.

MANUFACTURER: Nintendo

NUMBER OF PLAYERS: This is a 1-player, 1-Game Boy game.

CHARACTERS: You are the controller of the paddle.

CONTROL PAD:
Arrows: Move the paddle left or right.
"A" BUTTON: Releases the ball to start the game. Also, if the A **button** is pressed while the Left or Right arrow key is pressed, the paddle will move quicker.
"B" BUTTON: If the **B button** is pressed while the Left or Right arrow key is pressed, the paddle will move slower.

PAUSE
Press the **Start** button to pause the game; press the button again to resume play. The pause cannot be engaged during the bonus stage.

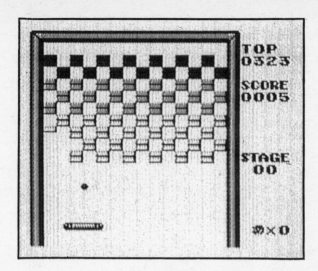

Lots of targets.

RESET

To reset the game, press the **Select** button at the same time as the **Start** button to return to the title screen.

NUMBER OF LEVELS

There are 24 stages plus 8 bonus screens for a total of 32 levels.

NUMBER OF LIVES

You start the game with 5 lives, and will lose one each time you miss the ball with the paddle. You will gain one life with each 1,000 points you score, up to a maximum of 9 remaining paddles. Once your score is over 10,000 points you will earn no new lives.

Mario hops on the paddle at the start of the game, and then hops off at the end.

SCORING POINTS

Each of the block types is worth a varying amount of points, as follows:

White. 1 point.
Gray. 2 points.
Black. 3 points.
Black/White Half-and-Half. Unbreakable.

When the ball hits a gray or black block, it will move faster.

TYPES OF SCREENS

There are four types of screens that the game will cycle through:

Basic Screen. This is the opening screen, with 7 rows of blocks at the top. The blocks are stationary.

Scrolling Block Screen. The rows of blocks at the top of the screen scroll from right to left or the other direction.

Advancing Block Screen. Sometimes the rows of blocks at the top of the screen will descend one row toward the paddle. If you can clear this screen, you will enter one of the bonus stages.

Bonus Stage. This is a timed level; your goal is to break as many blocks as possible within the allotted time. If you miss the ball, you will exit the bonus stage but not lose a life.

POWER PLAYER HINTS

Study the way the ball moves off the wall, ceiling or a block. It will return at the same angle.

Use the speedup and slowdown buttons (**A button** and **B button**) together with the Arrow keys. Learn to coordinate the speed of the paddle to the speed of the descending ball.

Ordinarily, the ball hitting the paddle will rebound at the same angle, just like the blocks, walls and ceilings. However, there are several special techniques you can use to put a bit of "English" on the ball:

Snapping the ball. Change the direction of the paddle at the moment it is hit by the ball.

Pushing the ball. Hit the ball with one end or the other of the moving paddle, shoving it toward the wall in the direction the paddle is moving.

Pull the ball. Move the paddle in a direction opposite that of the ball at the moment it is hit.

SPECIAL RULES

If your score is over 10,000 points, the onscreen display will recycle to 0000 and a special symbol will appear at the score location.

Alleyway is a trademark of Nintendo of America Inc. © 1989 Nintendo of America Inc.

Boomer's Adventure in Asmik World

AGE: 6 years to Adult
DIFFICULTY: Apprentice

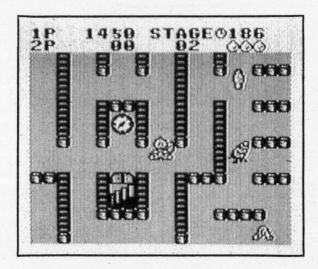

Go grab that compass!

There's no way to get around it. This game is . . . CUTE. It has a cute little star named Boomer. It has a cute, bouncy musical score. And the creatures that inhabit Asmik World may have threatening names and nasty habits, but there's no way around it: they're cute, too.

Here's the story: "Asmik World was a peaceful land inhabited by peaceful people who had evolved from dinosaurs. But one day, furious winds began to blow bringing rain which lasted for many months. The people were afraid that their peaceful land had come under an evil spell. One morning, their fears were realized when a giant tower appeared in the midst of their land, tall enough to pierce the clouds."

People evolved from dinosaurs? Well, okay, we can deal with that. Sounds cute.

Anyhow, the dinosaur people of Asmik go to the village seer who says that the rain and darkness were the fault of the evil lord Zoozoon, who seeks

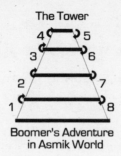

The Tower

Boomer's Adventure
in Asmik World

to rule the world from his tower. Many brave warriors of Asmik tried to challenge Zoozoon but never returned. But there is still one last hope: Boomer.

Boomer has to master 32 mazes up and 32 mazes down, avoiding attackers and finding the hidden key to unlock the door to the next stage. There's an enemy boss waiting at the end of each of the 8 worlds. Boomer's bag of tricks include the ability to dig holes to trap his pursuers (like the classic arcade and PC game, Lode Runner and the new Hyper Lode Runner cartridge for the Game Boy) as well as various freezers and flamers and other tools. As the game speeds up, you may also think of Asmik World as Pac-Man with weapons.

The on-screen display for Boomer's Adventure in Asmik World is actually a window into a much larger world. The portion seen on the Game Boy is about one-fourth of the level; as you move left, right, up or down, the window will shift.

The two-player game, which can be used only with the Video Link and a second game pak, allows two Boomers to fight the bad guys at the same time.

MANUFACTURER: Asmik Corporation of America / (213) 624-2447

NUMBER OF PLAYERS: 2 players with Video Link.

CHARACTERS: Boom! You're Boomer.

CONTROL PAD:
Arrows: Move Boomer up, down, left or right.

"A" BUTTON: Digs a hole in front of Boomer, or fills up a hole he is facing.

"B" BUTTON: Use items.

Select: Selects Spirit Item.

PAUSE

Press the Start button to pause the game; press the button again to resume play.

NUMBER OF WORLDS

There are 8 worlds, each with 8 stages, for a total of 64 stages *(see the picture of the tower)*. Boomer must work his way from the base of the tower to the top, destroy Zoozoon the Lord of Darkness who is waiting at the top, and then work his way back down to the ground.

THE HOLE STORY

Press the **A button** to put Boomer to work digging a hole in front of him. When the hole is finished, it will be filled with X marks; don't overdig or Boomer will begin to fill in the hole. Holes cannot overlap, and there must be room between Boomer and a wall or obstacle before digging can begin.

Boomer must be careful not to fall into his own holes; if he does, he will be trapped for a short while, losing points on the clock and running the risk of capture by an enemy.

Dig a hole in front of the path of an oncoming enemy and hope that he is stupid enough to walk right in. Once he has fallen in, you have two choices:

1. Walk over the top of the enemy, who will remain in the hole for a short while and cannot harm you while he is trapped, or
2. Fill in the hole over a trapped enemy to destroy him.

To fill a hole, Boomer must be facing it, standing slightly back from its opening.

TIMING

Each stage has a limited amount of time, with the clock displayed at the upper right corner of the screen. Lower levels begin with 200 ticks on the clock; we timed the game against a stopwatch and found that each tick is roughly equal to one second of real time, so early stages allow a liberal three-and-a-half minutes or so.

ENEMIES

We'll start with the minor annoyances who wriggle around from place to place in the maze.

Creepy. One of the more common at lower levels, he's joined in early stages by **Flippy,** who bears a distant family relationship to his eminence, Pac-Man. Other creatures are **Speedy, Barfy, Crawler, Snouts** and **Dodo.**

There are four bosses at the various levels of the game, plus the baddest of the bad, Zoozoon:

Bouncer. A fathead who wears dark sunglasses. He'll try to squish you with his heaviness.

Moth. He'll flitter around the maze spitting poison spores in your direction.

Beetle. Somewhere between a worm and an insect, it has a pair of claws. It can spit out a poisonous thread you'll want to avoid.

Spike. Even worse than your average porcupine, this guy has poison in his needles.

Zoozoon. The Dark Lord and Ruler of the Tower, this is one big, ugggly dude. But you tell him, not us.

POWER UP-ITEMS

Spread around the 64 levels of the tower are a number of special items that can assist Boomer in his quest to defeat Zoozoon. Some of the items can be found lying on the ground in the mazes, some are buried (dig it?) and some are held by an enemy and are revealed only when Boomer has trapped an enemy in a hole.

There are two types of special items; one enhances the action of the standard **A button,** while the others are available with the use of the **B button.** Here are the items:

DIGGING ITEMS

Shovel. Boomer will speed through his digging. **A button.**

Time Bomb. Allows Boomer to dig as many as five holes at once, or as a weapon against a nearby enemy. **B button.**

SPECIAL WEAPONS

Bone. Your very basic weapon. Boomer can use it once to destroy or disable an enemy.

Boomerang. Boomer can throw this weapon to destroy or disable an enemy up to three times. **B button.**

Chili Pie. That's one spicy pepper! When Boomer takes a bite, he can breathe fire and disable the enemy for a short period of time. **B button.**

Ice Cream. This is chilly of a different sort. When Boomer sinks his teeth into one of these, he gains the ability to freeze any nearby enemy. If Boomer kicks them while they're frozen, they will slide across the screen and break up into little pieces, taking the wall with them. Hmmm . . . that's a good way to knock down a wall that's in the way, isn't it? **B button.**

KEY-FINDERS

Compass. Press the **B button** and the direction of the compass needle will point the way to the hidden key. The compass can be used four times before it stops working.

Detector. This small radar device will beep as Boomer gets near the key. **A button.**

TRANSPORTATION

Roller Skates. Zzzzzoooom.

Ski Boots. Have you ever tried to run while wearing ski boots? These will slow Boomer down until he finds the next pair of roller skates.

SPECIAL SPECIAL ITEMS

There are two extra-special items found only on the top floor of the tower. One is an **Egg,** which gives Boomer an extra life. The second is **Spirit,** an icon that looks vaguely like some kind of fish. When Boomer is in possession of one of these, he can exchange it for any other special item; press the Select button until you see the item you want displayed in the upper right-hand corner of the screen, and then press either the **A button** or the **B button** to enter your selection.

POWER PLAYER HINTS

Get that Compass or the Detector. They are the easiest way to be pointed to the direction of the hidden key. Notice that sometimes the compass direction will change: this means that the key is on something that is moving! Like one of those creepy crawlers. Once you've spotted the guy with the key, keep your eye on him until you can track him down.

Watch to see if some of the pursuers give you a hint of a special item they are carrying before you trap them. For example, one of the enemies may briefly toss a compass in the air from time to time.

USING PASSWORDS

When you reach a stage with a boss, a password will appear on the screen. Write it down; it will allow you to resume the game at a later time from that point.

To enter a password, use the arrow keys to move the flashing cursor to select the letters from a menu. Press the **A button** to enter. If you make a mistake, use the arrow on the menu to move the cursor back to the letter in the password you want to change. Once the password is complete onscreen, press the Start button.

Boomer's Adventure in Asmik World is a trademark of Asmik Corp. of America. © 1990 Asmik Corp. of America.

Bubble Ghost

AGE: 6 years-Adult
DIFFICULTY: Apprentice-Hot Dog

A scene from the PC version of Bubble Ghost.

Preview

Bubble Ghost is a strange combination of some of the weirdest elements of Bubble Bobble and Dr. Chaos, with a little bit of Casper the Friendly Ghost mixed in.

As we finished this book, the programmers at FCI were hard at work creating a Game Boy version of Bubble Ghost; we took a look at the IBM

PC version of the game marketed by Accolade for a hint of the fun that is in store.

In the PC game, we find ourselves inside the haunted castle of the crazy inventor Heinrich Von Schtinker. The old guy met his untimely end while testing his electric bubble pipe in the bathtub, not a particularly bright place for such an experiment.

Old crazy Schtinker has been seen blowing a bubble through the halls of the castle. Your job is to help Bubble Ghost move the bubble through all 35 of the rooms of the castle, past the mad inventions of Von Schtinker, without blowing the bubble. These inventions can be pretty prickly characters, including spikes, knives, pins, needles scissors and shears.

The Bubble Ghost himself is indestructible, and can touch and cross over any object without injury. Not so tough is the bubble, which will burst if it touches any object. You start the PC game with 6 bubbles (5 in your Bubble Pouch plus the one you are blowing) but you can pick up some more.

To move the bubble, the Bubble Ghost must blow on it. The closer the ghost is to the bubble, the stronger the blow. But don't blow too long without stopping to let BG breathe, or he'll turn red in the face and you'll lose points. In addition to blowing the bubble, Bubble Ghost must blow on objects in the castle to clear the way for the bubble.

Hidden around the castle are a number of secret passageways and rooms that can only be discovered by blowing on the right object.

This game sounds just a little bit different from many of the other arcade games for the Nintendo Entertainment System and the Game Boy. And, its heritage is a bit unusual, too. It was designed and programmed by a French company called Infogrames, the same people who brought the game Pinball Wizard to the market.

IBM PC version: Bubble Ghost is a trademark of Accolade, Inc. Bubble Ghost was designed and programmed by Infogrames of France. IBM PC version © 1988 Accolade, Inc.

Bugs Bunny Crazy Castle

AGE: 5 years to Adult
DIFFICULTY: Apprentice-Hot Dog

Bugs . . . Bugs . . . Bugs! That's all folks, and this is one very nicely designed entertainment for the Game Boy. The game differs very little from the NES version of Bugs Bunny Crazy Castle, except that it seems even more playable with the close-to-the-hand-and-eye Game Boy.

Heading for the elevator.

Your goal is to pick up all of the carrots on each level without getting caught by one of your pursuers. You can run across the levels back and forth, or go up and down stairs. You'll also find doorways with arrows pointing up or down (one direction only) that you can use to go from floor to floor in each level.

Bugs Bunny can even survive dives off of the highest cliffs. In some of the upper levels, you will find floors that have pipes; you must go to the entrance of the pipes in order to go up or down. If you are caught, you will lose a life and have to start the level over again.

This game includes two features we very much like to see in a puzzle game. First of all it includes a Continue feature that allows you to play again once a level is over; you will resume at the start of the level in which you lost your last Bugs, although you will begin with zero points. The second feature is a password entry; write down the password for the highest level you have mastered before you turn off the power, and the next time you play the game you can jump right to that level to start.

We found this game to be a lot of fun and would strongly recommend it to fans of chase adventures like Super Marioland.

MANUFACTURER: Seika / (213) 373-8127

NUMBER OF PLAYERS: 1.

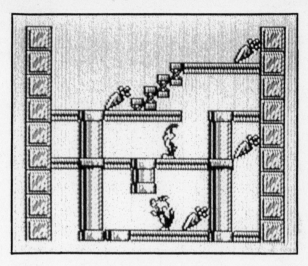

A pipe dream.

CHARACTERS

Well, there's Bugs Bunny. And a bunch of guys chasing him. (See Enemies.)

CONTROL PAD

Arrows: Used to move Bugs Bunny left or right, or up or down stairs or the pipes.

"A" or "B" BUTTONS: Used to throw the boxing glove at one of your pursuers.

PAUSE

Press the Start button to pause the game; press the button again to resume play.

NUMBER OF LIVES

Five to start. You will earn an extra life each time you complete a level.

SECRET WEAPONS

As you run around the castle, be on the lookout for some interesting special items that may be scattered about. These include:

Boxing Glove. Grab one, and wait for one of the bad guys to come at you. Press the **A or B button** and the glove will be thrown in the direction Bugs is facing. See Power Player Hints for a tip.

Magic Carrot Juice. Grab one, take a snort, and become invisible for a short time.

No Carrot Sign. Don't touch. You don't want to know.

Bucket, Safe, 10-ton Weight and **Wooden Crate.** Get behind one of these guys and push it off the floor and onto the heads of one of your pursuers.

ENEMIES

Daffy Duck, Sylvester, Wile E. Coyote and Yosemite Sam.

I ALWAYS WANTED TO KNOW

Okay, I'll bite. What happens if you touch the "No Carrot Sign?" You'll bite? Funny guy. Okay: if you touch the sign, you'll immediately be sent into a special, difficult level. If you can complete this level, you will win a bonus of three extra lives. If you fail, you will be dropped back three levels below the current one. Don't say we didn't warn you!

POWER PLAYER HINTS

A boxing glove once thrown can be grabbed again for another try. Just go to the left or right edge of the screen where the glove had been thrown and pick it up.

USING PASSWORDS

At the end of each completed level the game will display a four-letter password. Write down the code and save it for the next time you pick up the game and want to zoom to an advanced level.

We don't want to spoil the fun for you, but here are two codes that will bring you into Level 6, which is the first appearance of the pipes in the game, and Level 7, which is the first maze with multiple Sylvesters.

Level 6: SXES
Level 7: ZW4S

Remember that you won't need one in order to continue. Just choose the Continue option after your game is over.

In the password and the Continue modes, you will resume play with 0 points on the counter.

Hyper Lode Runner

AGE: 6 years-Adult
DIFFICULTY: Apprentice-Master of the Game

A pursuer drops into a hole.

Roaring from out of the past into the distant future on today's hottest new little game machine: It's Lode Runner, in a Game Boy version called Hyper Lode Runner.

Lode Runner was an old hit, one of the first and most clever video games in the early days of PCs. It has been updated and improved here, and Bandai's Game Boy version also includes an intriguing head-to-head competition that uses the Video Link.

There's a story line, if it's important to you: We're in the year 2264 on Earth, and the good old United World government has been overthrown in a bloody revolution lead by the renegade Red Lord of Darkness and his army of cyborgs. According to reports from spies, millions of political prisoners are being tortured in the Red Lord's infamous Labyrinth of Doom far beneath the surface of the planet. This brick-walled maze, guarded by a ruthless army of mutant cyborg zombies (are there any other kind?) includes millions in stolen gold.

Your assignment, should you accept it, is to make your way down into the maze and come back out with enough gold to finance the counter-revolution.

Enough of the story: trust us, this is a clever and addictive little game, and well suited to the Game Boy. It's also a bit difficult to describe: we think of Hyper Lode Runner as an action maze game. You have to solve problems such as how to get from Point A to Point B; you also have to figure out how to get there without getting eaten or beaten by a bad guy. And there's a bit of arcade action with Lode Runner's trap-digging abilities.

The object of the game is to capture all of the gold on a particular level and then escape. Some of the gold is just lying around; some of it is buried beneath bricks you will have to dig up, and some of the gold is being carried around by your pursuers (the mutant cyborg zombies, remember?) When you've collected all of the gold on a level, a hidden ladder will be exposed, and you can scurry up it and out of one level and into the next. There are also hidden keys that can open locked doors to back rooms.

The Lode Runner can dig up any brick he comes across, but cannot remove any solid blocks beneath his feet. Bricks can be removed to make temporary openings to retrieve hidden blocks, or they can be taken away to make a trap for a cyborg.

The game also includes a pair of very important anti-boredom features. We especially like the ability to create your own challenges using the "Edit" facility of the game. And you can also select a starting level from the first 16 stages of the game.

MANUFACTURER: Bandai / (213) 926-0947

NUMBER OF PLAYERS
1, or 2 players connected with Video Link cable. Two-player game requires two copies of Hyper Lode Runner game.

CHARACTERS
You are the last of the great Lode Runners.

CONTROL PAD
Arrows: Move the Lode Runner left or right. Use the Up arrow to climb a ladder. Use the Down arrow to descend a ladder, or to drop from a ladder to the surface.

"A" BUTTON: Digs bricks to the right of the Lode Runner.

"B" BUTTON: Digs bricks to the left of the Lode Runner.

Select: The Self-Destruct button. Press this button if the Lode Runner is hopelessly trapped; the game will restart from the same level.

If you press the Select button while the game is paused, the entire level you are on can be viewed.

Select + Start: Press the Select and Start buttons together to reset the game.

PAUSE

To pause the game, press the Start button; press the button again to resume play.

NUMBER OF LIVES

You will lose a life each time you are touched by one of the pursuing cyborgs.

If you fall into a pit between two bricks, you are trapped and must give up.

You will gain a new life each time you clear a level; the maximum number of lives you can possess at any one time is 8.

HOW TO CAPTURE THE BEASTIES

Dig a trap in front of an oncoming cyborg and wait for him to fall into it. When he does, he may expose a piece of gold he has been carrying. Run right across the top of his head before he wriggles out of the trap.

The holes you dig will automatically fill themselves in after a short while; if your hole is too fresh, a cyborg may fall in and eventually crawl out. If the cyborg falls in a stale hole, it will fill in around him and destroy him.

SCORING POINTS

Each piece of gold you collect is worth 150 points.

Each key you grab is worth 250 points.

You'll earn a cool 500 points, plus an additional Lode Runner, for each level you completely clear.

VS. MODE

Select the VS mode to set up a head-to-head competition between two Game Boy players. Each contestant must have his own copy of the Hyper Lode Runner game, and the Game Boys must be connected by a Video Link cable.

The goal of the VS game is for each player to clear out a particular level before his opponent does, finishing the assignment before the clock at the bottom center of the screen runs out of time.

There are several special VS mode objects. The following two items are hidden in some of the stacks of gold:

Freeze. Slows down the movements of your opponent.
Attack. Makes all of your opponent's gold disappear.

If you destroy a robot in VS play, up to three additional robots will appear on your opponent's screen.

Special scoring to VS mode is as follows:

Gold (Normal). 150 points
Gold (Bonus). 300 points
Clearing a Stage. 3,000 points.

EDIT MODE

In the Edit Mode, you will be able to create your own Hyper Lode Runner screen. Your special challenge will remain in the system until you turn off the power.

When the title screen is displayed, select Edit and press the Start button. Choose the screen you want to edit from the eight available choices. They are numbered from 1A to 4B. Screens ending with an A are front rooms; those ending with a B are back rooms.

Use the arrow keys to move the onscreen cursor to the object you want to move. Press the B button to select an object; press the A button to install the object at the location of the flashing cursor.

Available objects are:

Bricks
Gold
Robot
Player
Ladder
Escape Ladder

USING PASSWORDS

You do not need a password to enter any of the first 16 levels, which can be chosen at the start of the game. To jump into a stage beyond the first 16, write down the password you will receive as you complete each advanced level.

Lock 'N Chase

AGE: 6 years-Adult
DIFFICULTY: Novice-Apprentice

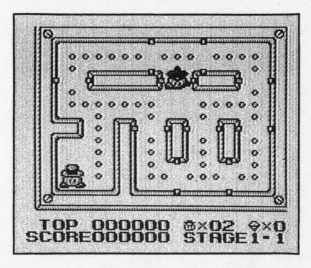

The opening maze.

It's very hard to write about this game without mentioning the "P" word. We'll try, though.

Lock 'N Chase is an entertaining maze chase game, well suited to the small scale of the Game Boy. You know, kind of like Pa . . . oops.

The story line is this: you're a clever thief trying to pull off the diamond heist of the century. You do this by racing around the corridors and alleyways of a six-level maze, gobbling up coins. Just like Pac (sorry).

All the time as you run through this maze, you're being chased by cops. Some of them are fast, some of them are slow and some of them are not too bright, but the farther you go into the maze the more of them there are and the more pesky they become. We wonder how Pac-Ma . . . Yipes! We almost said Pac-Man.

Oh well, we give up. Lock 'N Chase is an enhanced and improved version of the venerable Pac-Man game, which is not a bad family tree to branch off of. There are some nice additions to the basic idea, including the ability to place temporary barriers in the mazes to isolate some of your pursuers, bonus stage slot machines and a nifty stereo sound track.

Your ultimate goal is to snare the African Star Diamond, hidden six levels deep into Lock 'N Chase.

This game won't challenge the mind like some of the brain bogglers like Kwirk, Ishido or Boxxle, but it is a very entertaining challenge.

MANUFACTURER: Data East / (408) 286-7074

NUMBER OF PLAYERS: 1.

CHARACTERS: You are a tiny little thief.

CONTROL PAD
Arrows: Move your character Up, Down, Left or Right on the maze.
"A" or "B" BUTTONS: Puts up barriers behind you when police are chasing you.

PAUSE
Press the Start button to pause the game; press the button again to resume play. While the game is in pause, you can use the arrow keys to pan the screen to check out your options.

NUMBER OF LIVES
You start the game with three lives. You will lose a life each time you are caught by the police. You can gain an extra life by matching all three icons in the Bonus Stage Slot Machine.

SPECIAL ITEMS
There are a number of special items and special bonuses to be had along the way in your chase. They include:

Coins. You must collect all of the coins that are scattered about on the maze pathways. Each coin is worth 10 points.
Money Bags. First of all, each time you grab one of these bags, the pursuing police will freeze in their tracks for a few seconds, allowing you to make an escape or grab a few coins you could not otherwise reach. In addition, bonus points are awarded, as follows:

First Money Bag.	500 points
Second Money Bag.	1000 points

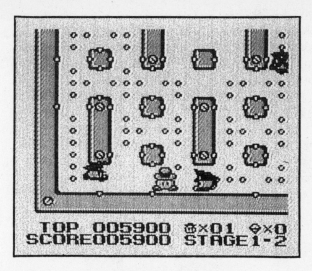

A portion of a larger maze.

Third Money Bag.	2000 points
Fourth Money Bag.	4000 points

Spinning Diamonds. Ah, the magic elixir of invincibility. Grab one of these and you will become untouchable for a while. And, for every diamond you collect you get to play the Bonus Round Slot Machine once at the end of each stage. Points for each diamond are as follows:

First Diamond.	100 points
Second Diamond.	200 points
Third Diamond.	500 points
Fourth or More.	1000 points

To play the Bonus Round Slot Machines, press the Start button to spin the wheels. To stop each window, press the **A or B button.**

Barriers. You can erect temporary barriers behind you to block the pursuit of police; they will disappear after a short while. No more than two barriers can be put in place at one time. If you manage to completely isolate a policemen between a pair of barriers, points are given as follows:

First time.	200 points
Second time.	500 points
Third time.	1000 points
Fourth time.	2000 points

If you can collect 10,000 points you will automatically be zoomed into the next higher stage.

POWER PLAYER HINTS

Leave sleeping policemen alone.

Don't assume that a closed door is one you can never get through.

There's a special tool you will need in order to get to the African Star Diamond.

POWER ZOOMING

There are unlimited Continues available at the end of each game. When the game is over, you will be returned to the title screen. To start over at the beginning of the game, press the Start button. To resume play at the beginning of the level you were in when the game ended, press the Select button to choose Continue and then press the Start button.

Lock 'N Chase is a trademark of Data East Corp. © 1990 Data East Corp.

Miner 2049er

AGE: 6 years-Adult
DIFFICULTY: Apprentice-Hot Dog

In a cavern, in a canyon, excavating for a mine, lived a miner, 49er, and his daughter Clementine.

The old song refers to the sad story of a California Gold Rush miner of the year 1849. This Game Boy entertainment is a version of a popular computer game that presumably refers to a miner from the next century after this one.

Your view of the game is from the front, as if the walls of the mine have been cut away. In order to finish a level, the miner has to walk on all of the territory on all of the ledges—some of them are easier to get to than others. As you walk across them, their appearance will change; some levels will require more than one pass.

Scattered about on the ledges are little mutant creatures that look sort of like bedraggled cats; touching them will cost you a life.

The miner can pick up various special items in the mine, including gems, hammers, medals, keys and canteens. While in possession of some of the special items, the miner can walk right by some of his tormentors.

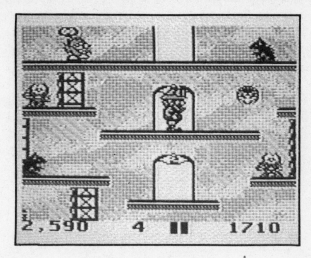

The Miner 2049er maze.

One of the real tricks of the game is to learn just how far a player can jump without getting killed. In general, a jump to the level below is okay, but more than one level can be lethal.

Players should also look for patterns for each of the levels to clear the screen within the available time.

We worked with early preproduction materials for the game.

MANUFACTURER: Mindscape / (708) 480-8715

NUMBER OF PLAYERS: 1 or 2.

CHARACTERS
You're the miner, 49er. No sign of Clementine.

CONTROL PAD
Arrows: Left and Right move the miner in those directions. Press Up to enter a transporter. Press Down to help guide the miner in mid-jump.

"A" BUTTON: Jumps. The miner can be guided in midair using the arrow keys.

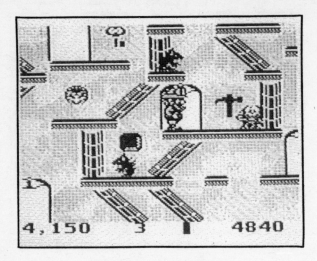

Another view of the maze.

NUMBER OF LEVELS

There are 10 levels to the mine, each with somewhat different types of challenges. The levels are:

The Slides. The miner can walk up ladders to reach higher levels, or go down ladders to slides to lower points.

Transporters. Use the elevator.

Calisthenics. There's a secret exit here somewhere.

Utility Hoist. Ride the small crane that hangs from the ceiling of the screen.

Suction Tubes. Swwooooosshh! You'll ride on air from one part of the mine to another like a piece of mail. There are also moving platforms to take you from one ledge to another on the same level. Don't dawdle: this is a short-time-period level.

Bob's Playroom. Slides and transporters and other sorts of fun things. Another short-time level.

Jumping 101. You've got to jump from ledge to ledge, of course.

Yukon's Penthouse. Fully equipped, it comes with ladders, slides and places to jump.

Luxury Transportation. All sorts of ways to zoom from place to place on screen, plus slides. A short-time level.

Acid Rain. Slides and moving platforms. Watch out for the rain; if a drop hits you, you will lose a life.

Motocross Maniacs

AGE: 6-Adult
DIFFICULTY: Apprentice-Master of the Game

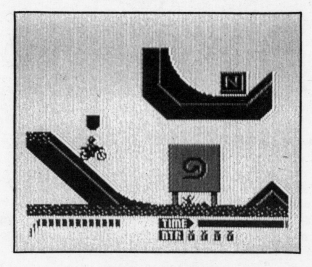

Heading into a ramp.

This is your chance to do all of those things your mother has warned you against. Zoom your bike across a gaping chasm; ride it up the side of a tube and down the other.

This game stars vehicles called World Class Dirt Bikes, believe it or not.

There are hidden power-ups scattered around the course, including Nitro Boosters and Time Extenders as well as a Jet to leave the earth entirely. You'll find the hidden items when you do a flip at the location of hidden items.

There are eight layouts in the cartridge; you can compete solo, against a computer-directed challenger or in a head-to-head race against a friend connected with the Video Link.

MANUFACTURER: Ultra Software Corp. / (708) 215-5111

NUMBER OF PLAYERS: 1, or 2 players using two game paks, a pair of Game Boys and the Video Link cable.

CHARACTERS

You are Motohead, whatever that is. If you are playing against the computer, your opponent will be Crashin' Vernin (Level A), Skeeter Skid Mark (Level B) or Izzy Insanity (Level C).

MODES

Lone Wolf Solo Mode. One player races against the clock. You must make it around the track faster than the Qualifying TIme Clock in order to advance to the next lap.

Computer Challenge Mode. You're up against the merciless computer driver here. You've got to race against the other bikes as well as the Qualifying Time Clock.

Two-player Mode. A down-and-dirty handlebar-to-handlebar challenge between two Game Boys, connected by a Video Link cable.

CONTROL PAD

Arrows: Move the bike up, down, left or right on the track.

Press and hold the Up arrow during a jump, your bike will stay in the air longer.

Press the Right arrow while your bike is in midair, and your bike will flip.

Press the Left arrow while on the ground to tip backward and pop a Wheelie.

"A" BUTTON: The **A button** is the bike's throttle. Press it to adjust your speed and gears.

"B" BUTTON: The **B button** is the Nitro Turbo Boost Button. Zzzzoooommmmm! Each time you use this afterburner, though, you will use up a nitro canister or a gallon of jet propulsion fuel, both of which are in limited supply.

PAUSE

Press the Start button to pause the game; press the button again to resume play.

Flying without wings.

NUMBER OF TRACKS

There are 8 different tracks, ranging from the relatively simple Track 1, also known as the Bunny Course, to the (almost) impossible Track 8.

NUMBER OF LEVELS

In the Solo and Computer Challenge versions of the game, there are three available levels: Easy (A), Bumpy (B) and Crazy (C).

TIMING

Your goal is to complete two laps on the course, finishing at least as fast as the qualifying time or the time of your opponent. The game cartridge presents this information in a rather confusing way, and the manual is of no help at all. What you will see on screen once you have picked a Course and Level is a display that will tell you the Course Record and the Qualifying Time. The qualifying time is the speed you must complete *one lap* in order to make a try at the second lap of a race; the course record is the fastest official time for *two laps*.

If you are at all like us, it will be quite a while before you can advance into some of the upper levels. For example, the Bunny Course 1 allows you 1:20 (one minute and 20 seconds) for completion of one lap at the A level, which is challenging enough. The same course at the C level gives only 16 seconds for completion of one level.

Here are the course records and qualifying times for each of the courses and levels in Motocross Maniacs:

Course	Level	Course Record	Qualifying Time
1	A	2:02	1:20
2	A	1:56	1:25
3	A	1:52	1:19
4	A	1:58	1:12
5	A	2:04	1:44
6	A	1:57	1:28
7	A	1:59	1:29
8	A	2:03	1:18
1	B	2:02	0:45
2	B	1:56	0:50
3	B	1:52	0:59
4	B	1:58	0:35
5	B	2:04	1:05
6	B	1:57	0:50
7	B	1:59	0:45
8	B	2:03	1:05
1	C	2:02	0:16
2	C	1:56	0:26
3	C	1:52	0:32
4	C	1:58	0:14
5	C	2:04	0:45
6	C	1:57	0:30
7	C	1:59	0:25
8	C	2:03	0:35

SCORING POINTS

The top scores for the current session are recorded in the Game Boy's memory, but will be erased when power is turned off.

SECRET WEAPONS

There are a number of special items scattered about on the course. Unlike a real race course, on this one you're *supposed* to try to run over things in your way. Hit the following:

Jet Propulsion Fuel. Look for the Js to fuel your Turbo Booster. Jump into these in mid-air.

Mini-Maniacs. Hitchhikers you'll find along the way. They'll come out when you do somersaults at certain secret spots.

Nitro Turbo Boosts. Cans of instant pep-up for your bike. Look for the Ns.

Radial Tires. Super-traction tires keep your bike from slip, sliding away in the mud and hills. When you have the extra rubber, the word "TIRE" will be displayed in the lower left corner of the screen. R is for Radial.

Speed Multiplier. Special Ss send super speed. (Once your speedometer is maxxed out, you can't go any faster even if you pick up a few extra of these, though.)

Bonus Time. Have a couple of Ts whenever you can; they are the *only* way to complete some levels. Each one you snag adds 10 seconds to your time limit.

I ALWAYS WANTED TO KNOW

How do I get over those rocks that are placed in the middle of the course? Here's where a Wheelie will come in handy. Try combining the wheelie with a Nitro boost to zoom up and over the obstacles. Practice your wheelies (Left arrow) until you can do them on command, under control. Otherwise, they will be nothing more than spectacular, dangerous wastes of your time.

DANGER!

This is no ride in the park, as you will quickly discover. It's actually closer to an amusement park roller coaster. Here are some of the obstacles you will find on the courses:

Bowl-Dacious. Stay out of the soup. They'll knock you down every time if you try to drive over them.

Head-Spinning Loops. Special attractions here include double loops, ceiling loops and hop, skip and jump loops.

Hop-a-Long Jumps. A series of small or large jumps. You'll have to get the timing just right to come down past them or between them.

Macho Dirt. Rough and tough patches of dirt that will slow you down considerably when you try to slog through them.

Rock and a Hard Place. These are the boulders strewn about, especially in upper courses. Use a wheelie and a nitro boost, and be sure to wear your helmet.

Sky Riding Ramp. These ramps are almost everywhere—especially in the upper levels. They may be the only way to get over a slow or treacherous area, and they are also often the hiding place for the special items you will need.

Stop Gaps. This course is still under construction, or should be. You'll have to maintain enough speed to fly over the gaps or obstacles.

POWER PLAYER HINTS

Learn the location of two very important special items. The Ts give you 10 seconds of bonus time, which may be the only way you will ever win some of the more difficult courses. The Ns are Nitro Turbo Boosts, and they'll give your bike the extra pep it needs to get through slow spots and up into the ramps where many of the bonus items are stored.

Nemesis

AGE: 6 years-Adult
DIFFICULTY: Apprentice-Master of the Game

First of all, let's get one thing straight here: that's not a Game Boy you hold in your hand. It's a Proteus 911 Control Panel.

And you—you are the chief of the Interplanetary Police. You're out on patrol in what has to be the most Rad police cruiser ever: the Proteus 911. You're off on the pursuit of the evil King Nemesis in a shoot-em-up in space in the nice translation of an arcade hit to the tiny Game Boy screen.

And what a long strange trip it'll be. You'll visit scenic Carnage Canyon, the famed Pyramids of Pyromania, the romantic Lair of the Planetary Pirates, the cheery Den of Doom and Gloom and the tourist-trekked Sacrificial Sarcophagus of Saturn.

We especially like the setup screen of this little game which allows the player to customize a great deal. And we appreciate the fact that a player can grant himself no less than 100 Continues.

MANUFACTURER: Ultra Software / (708) 215-5111

NUMBER OF PLAYERS: 1

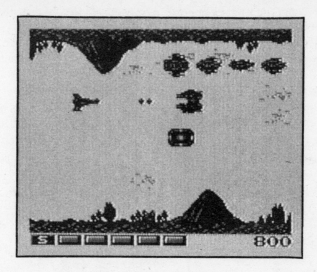

Your basic outerspace shoot-em-up.

CHARACTERS

Congratulations! You are the chief of the Interplanetary Police. We're sorry to inform you, though, that the evil King Nemesis has placed a billion dollar bounty on your head.

CONTROL PAD

Arrows: The arrows are used to move the Proteus up, down, right (forward) or left (reverse) across the scrolling landscape.

"A" BUTTON: Press to fire weapons. (Note that the assignments of the **A and B buttons** can be switched as one of the options of the configuration screen.)

"B" BUTTON: Press for Power-ups.

PAUSE

Press the Start button to pause the game; press the button again to resume play.

NUMBER OF WORLDS

There are five stages in the game. They are all left-to-right scrolling scenes with oncoming alien fighters. The difference comes with the various backgrounds and obstacles. We particularly liked Stage 3, which has versions of the famously weird carved head statues of Easter Island scattered about.

The levels each have their own neat Nemesis names:

Level 1: Carnage Canyon
Level 2: Pyramids of Pyromania
Level 3: Lair of the Planetary Pirates
Level 4: Den of Doom and Gloom
Level 5: Sacrificial Sarcophagus of Saturn

There are also a number of Bonus Stages hidden in various parts of the game; you'll come across them as you cruise through space. Once you're in a Bonus Stage, look for special Bonus Capsules marked with a "B". If you can capture all of the bonus capsules in succession, you will receive a huge point bonus.

Also in the Bonus Stage are 1-Up Capsules (a circle with a 1) that increase your number of remaining ships by one for each that you capture.

NUMBER OF LEVELS

You can choose one of two levels from the configuration screen. Level 2 sends more enemies, faster.

NUMBER OF LIVES

In the standard game, you begin your adventure with three lives. An unusual feature of this game is the ability to set your own level of lives, from 1 to 100.

CONFIGURATION

One of the most unusual features of Nemesis is the Configuration screen, where you can adjust many of the parameters of the game. Here are the choices:

Stage. Select from 1 through 5 as your starting point.
Level. Select 1 (easiest) or 2 (more difficult).
Rest. Here you can choose the number of extra fighters you will have at the beginning of the game. Use the left or right arrow key to move the number lower or higher. A setting of 00 limits you to the single fighter you have at the start; a setting of 99, the highest, gives you a total of 100 fighters.
Auto Shot. Use the left or right arrow to toggle between ON and OFF. When Auto Shot is on, your fighter will shoot bursts of missiles; when Auto Shot is off, the gun will fire just once each time the firing button is pressed.

Shot/Power-Up. Here you can assign the functions of the A and B buttons. The game is originally set up so that the **A button** fires the currently selected weapon and the **B button** upgrades your fighter using one of the power-ups you have collected. Use the left or right arrow to toggle between the standard setting and a reversed setting.

Once you have completed your configuration, press the Start button to begin the game.

SECRET WEAPONS

There are many special items strewn about in space.

As you destroy enemies, many of them will leave behind a small power-up capsule on screen. Each time you touch one of the capsules, the indicator at the bottom left corner of the screen will move from one setting to the next—from S to M to D to L to O to F and back to the beginning again. You can engage the special weapon of your choice by waiting until the one you want is indicated and then press the **B button.** Your **A button** will now be enhanced until the next time you press the **B button** or lose a life.

Here are the meanings of the various power-up symbols:

S. Speed Burner. Boosts your speed all the way to Warp 3.

M. Missiles. Adds two All-Terrain Attack Missiles to your arsenal.

D. Double Gun. A directional beam that sends out projectiles in front and above your fighter at the same time.

L. Laser. Gives you a long-distance laser gun weapon.

O. Option. Gives you a second, shadow fighter plane that will double your firepower.

F. Force Field. A barrier that will protect you from oncoming enemy weapons for three hits, after which it will disappear.

In addition, look for the following special weapon:

Enemy Annihilation Capsule. Scarf up one of these hubcap-like capsules for instant relief: it will clear all of the enemies on the screen when you grab it.

See the description of the Bonus Stage in the Number of Worlds section above for information about the special Bonus Capsules and 1-Up Capsules hidden there.

ENEMIES

As befits any decent alien, each has his, her or its own fearsome name. Here are some of them:

Coda. A coda is a finishing touch to a piece of music; stay away from this gigantic space urchin to avoid an untimely finish to your own song.

Moal. The Easter Island stone statue himself.

Each of the five levels is ruled by its own ultimate alien boss:

Level 1. Intergalactic Super Force.

Level 2. Venus Destructo.

Level 3. Super Alien.

Level 4. Assassination Tower.

Level 5. King Nemesis's Ultimate Hideout.

Nemesis is a registered trademark of Crystalline Creations, Inc. Ultra and Ultragames are registered trademarks of Ultra Software Corp. Game pak © 1990 Ultra Software Corp.

Paperboy
AGE: 6 years-Adult
DIFFICULTY: Apprentice-Master of the Game

Bad news.

It sure beats peddling up and down the hills of San Francisco with a heavy sack of newspapers on your back. All you've got to do is twiddle your thumbs on the Game Boy version of the arcade and NES hit, Paperboy.

You've got to steer your bicycle down the street, remembering which houses are customers and which ones are not. You've got to watch out for oncoming cars, nasty dogs and overhanging trees. And there are lawn ornaments, fire hydrants and sewer grates.

Oh yes, we forgot a few: tornados, break dancers, tombstones and the Grim Reaper.

Yes, Paperboy the game is not your ordinary route.

This Game Boy cartridge is nearly identical to the full-sized NES, with the obvious difference of the monochrome and lower-resolution Game Boy screen. On the plus side is a super stereo version of the familiar dah-dah-dah-dadadada Paperboy musical theme (it gets a bit repetitive after a while, though) and some neat sound effects including the satisfying thwack of a paper against a door, the tinkle of broken glass or the sickening thud of a collision with an oncoming truck.

Your job as paperboy is to deliver your stack of "The Daily Sun" papers to your subscribers. At the start of each round of the game, you'll see a map of the neighborhood with your subscribers indicated in light colors. Dark houses are nonsubscribers.

As you steer your bike up the road, dodging obstacles, your aim is to land your Daily Suns in the newspaper paperbox of subscribers. You'll get the most points for popping those papers right into the box, fewer points for merely landing one on the porch or just hitting the door.

But, while you're at it, you can break the windows of nonsubscribers and otherwise cause havoc at the homes of people who don't pay for your services.

At the end of each day's deliveries, you enter into the Paperboy Training Course, a delivery boy's boot camp. Here you get to pick up some extra points while you hone your skills by tossing papers at targets and avoiding obstacles.

MANUFACTURER: Mindscape / (708) 480-8715

NUMBER OF PLAYERS

1 or 2. In a two-player game, the contestants alternate turns, using the same Game Boy.

CHARACTERS: You're the Paperboy.

CONTROL PAD

Arrows: Left or right arrows move the boy and his bicycle left or right. Pressing the Up arrow will speed up the bike; pressing the Down arrow

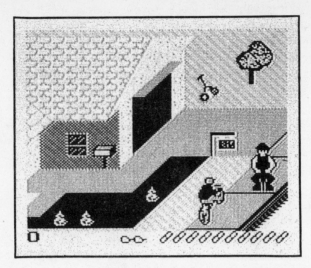

Heading for a crash.

will throw on the brakes. Letting go of the arrow keys will result in a gradual slowdown.

"A" or "B" BUTTONS: Press either button to throw a paper.

PAUSE

Press the **Start** button to pause the game; press the button again to resume. The pause command may not work in some sections of the game where there are digitized sound effects; wait for the sound to stop and then press **Start** again.

NUMBER OF WORLDS

There are seven days in a week, and you've got to get up at the crack of dawn every day to deliver your papers. Each of the rounds in the game is identified as a day of the week.

NUMBER OF NEWSPAPERS

You start out with a bundle of 10, which is not enough. You'll need to look for the little stacks of papers scattered on the front lawns of some of the houses on your route; run over the stack to pick up a new supply.

NUMBER OF LIVES

Four to begin with. You'll lose one life each time you crash and fall down, are hit by a truck or otherwise fail to complete your paper route.

NUMBER OF SUBSCRIBERS

At the end of each day's run, you'll receive your Daily Report from your supervisor. He'll inform you of complaints from subscribers; any who did not get their papers will cancel. Then you'll start the next day's deliveries with your list of remaining customers.

TIMING

Your pass down the streets is not timed, however the training course at the end of each day's work is limited to 45 ticks of the clock. If you can complete the course in that time or less, the number of seconds remaining will be multiplied times 100 and added to your score.

SCORING POINTS

Tossing the paper into a subscriber's paperbox	750
Tossing the paper onto a subscriber's porch	300
Breaking the window of a non-subscriber	300
Hitting a bush, tombstone, lamp or garbage can	300
Hitting a round target on the training course	200
Hitting a box target on the training course	100
Picking up an extra bundle of papers	50

In the Training Course, you will receive the following extra points *if you complete the course:*

Knocking over garbage cans*	300
Hitting targets*	200
Knocking over tombstones*	100
Remaining seconds on the clock, multiplied times	100.

HIGH SCORE SCREEN

If you make it into the Top 10 scorers, you will be given the opportunity to enter your initials on the high-score screen. Use the arrow pad Up or Down to scroll through the alphabet; when you see the letter you wish to enter, press either the A or B button to select. Press the Right arrow pad to move to the next letter.

OBSTACLES AND ENEMIES:

Breakdancers	Manholes
Cars	Motorcycles
Dog Houses	Skateboarding Fiends
Dogs	The Grim Reaper
Fences	Tires

Fire Hydrants	Tombstones
Garbage Cans	Tornados
Grates	Trees
Lawn Ornaments	Tricycles
Lawnmowers	Workmen

POWER PLAYER HINTS

Try to stay on the sidewalk; it's safer. But if someone or something ends up in your way—and you know this will happen—ride on the lawns of the houses or dart out into the street.

Keep an eye on the number of remaining newspapers in your bag (a display in the upper left corner of the screen shows how many are left). If you see a pile of replacement papers on a lawn ahead, throw all of your remaining papers at the homes of nonsubscribers to pick up some points.

In the Training Course, ride up the ramps to replenish your supply of newspapers.

Paperboy is a trademark of Atari Game Corp. © 1990, 1984 Tengen. Game pak © 1990 Mindscape, Inc.

Penguin Wars
AGE: 6 years-Adult
DIFFICULTY: Apprentice

Here is an unusual translation from a Japanese coin arcade game to the handheld Game Boy. This game is kind of like your basic bowling/shuffle-board/bocce game played by a penguin, cow, rabbit, bat or rat. You know, the sort of thing you see down at the playground every day.

The object of the game is to roll the most out of 10 balls onto the opposite side of the play screen within a 60-second period. Sounds simple enough to us, except that the other player will attempt to roll the balls back.

There are three games in a set, with the first player to win two games the winner.

If each player ends up with 5 balls on his side when time runs out, it is declared a Draw. If one player manages to get all 10 balls onto the other side within the time limit, it is called a Perfect Game.

MANUFACTURER: Nexoft / (213) 540-4778

NUMBER OF PLAYERS

1 player in the basic game. From 2 to 10 players can compete in a tournament using the Video Link.

CHARACTERS

Hey, what else? A penguin. Or, if you prefer, a rabbit, a cow, a bat or a rat.

CONTROL PAD

Arrows: In game play, the Left or Right arrows will move your character in those directions.

During the setup, the Up and Down arrows are used to choose the game mode and select a character.

"A" BUTTON: Press this button once to pick up the ball; press the button a second time to release the ball.

You can increase the speed of the ball by holding down the **A button** for a few seconds before releasing it. Be careful, though, not to hold down the button too long, or you will drain all of your character's energy and make it fall down.

If your character falls down, or is knocked down by your opponent's ball, you must press the **A button** repeatedly to get him back on his feet.

"B" BUTTON: Not used in this game.

PAUSE

Press the Start button to pause the game in single player mode only; press the button again to resume play.

SINGLE PLAYER GAME

You can choose from one of five characters, each with unique abilities:

Penguin. An all-around player of average ability, someone you can count on.

Cow. The strongest physical player, a bit slow but with a lot of muscle. The cow recovers the quickest when she is knocked down.

Rabbit. A goofy guy, he can hop around quickly and is a lot of fun, but is otherwise merely average.

Bat. A tough competitor, he is very quick and hard to hit; on offense he is a very good bowler.

Rat. A clever critter, he makes up for his small size and slow ball rolling with some exceptional strategy and determination.

Use the arrow keys to highlight one character and then press the **A button** to lock in your choice. The computer will then tell you the identity of the character it will use in competition against you.

Your chosen character will then compete against the four remaining characters, which will be under the control of the computer. If you succeed in defeating your opponent (by winning two out of three sets) the computer will introduce you to your next challenger.

ENEMIES

When remaining time reaches 20 seconds, you can expect to meet some special characters who will cause some extra special problems, trying to disrupt the balls that you will roll across the game table. They roam from right to left:

The Slime Monster. Balls will bounce straight back at you.

The Roving Ball. Attracts your ball and changes its course, rebounding it to you at an unpredictable angle.

The Spinning Disk. Makes the ball bounce almost anywhere.

The Crazy Dog. When he gets angry, your ball will come right back at you.

BONUS GAME

If you manage to score a Perfect Set (two Perfect Games) you will enter into a special bonus game. Here you will be given 30 seconds to roll as many balls across the table as you can before time runs out.

GAME SCREEN

The game screen will show you your current score and the highest score achieved in the current session. Also displayed is the remaining time for the game in progress. To the right of the onscreen playing table you will see a display of pegs that indicate the number of games each player has won in the current set.

SCORING POINTS

Each ball is worth 100 points. If you manage to hit your opponent with a ball, you will receive 1,000 points. If you can score a Perfect Set, you have the chance to earn extra points in a Bonus Round.

VIDEO LINK TOURNAMENT PLAY

From 2 to 10 players can enter into a Penguin Wars tournament. You'll need two Game Boys, two Penguin Wars game paks and a Video Link cable.

Both machines must be turned on and connected before one player selects the VS game.

The character selection screen will be displayed on both screens; use the arrow keys to indicate the character you want to start with and then press the **A button** to lock in your choice. You will also be able to enter your own name onto the screen, which will be very useful in a tournament that may include as many as 10 contestants. When the names of all of the players have been entered, press the Start button.

Once the entry of the names of players is completed, the Game Boy will display the tournament roster with the matchups for all of the sets. If there is an odd number of players (3, 5, 7 or 9), one player is "seeded" and will enter the tournament at a later point.

Playing the tournament game is identical to a standard two-player game. The first contestant in a pair to win two games wins a set and then the next pair play the game. Once every pair has played a set, a new tournament roster will be displayed with the next round of competition.

Penguin Wars is a trademark of Nexoft Corporation. © 1990 Nexoft Corporation; © 1985 ASCII Corporation.

Revenge of the 'Gator—Super Pinball

AGE: 6 to Adult
DIFFICULTY: Apprentice-Hot Dog

Pinball has come a long, long, long way from the old mechanical table units to the tiny handheld Game Boy. With Revenge of the 'Gator, it is fair to say that pinball has moved into the next generation.

We can't say enough about the quality of game play that is packed into the tiny Game Boy game pak here. There are eight screens, wondrous animation and response, a clever bouncy soundtrack, all of the beeps and buzzes you would expect from a pinball game and a nice sense of humor. This is a *great* game for the Game Boy, worth a couple of hours of play on a long airplane trip, car ride or just sitting on the sofa.

There are four levels of pinball screens in the game—you'll start in the second one up from the bottom. The second and third screens are connected to the screens above and below, and the bottom one is connected to the second screen at the top and a chute straight into the mouth of a hungry

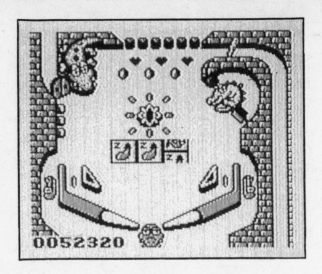

Watch out for those eggplants!

'Gator at the bottom. (He makes a convincing "gulp" when he swallows your ball.

The beauty of this design is that once you get the ball in play at the top level, you are three drops away from the 'Gator. It is quite easy to play one round for five or ten minutes in this game, unusual in a pinball game.

One of the best things about this game is the fact that it does not just kill off the new player immediately; even the worst of players should have 30 seconds or so before the gator gets fed. And, inside of about half an hour, we obtained scores of more than 300,000 points without even coming close to mastery of the game.

There are special "savers" that will appear from time to time, blocking off the exits at the bottoms and sides. They'll help you concentrate on your primary assignment of climbing up through the levels of the pinball game without having to worry about the hungry 'Gator down below.

MANUFACTURER: Hal America / (503) 644-4117

NUMBER OF PLAYERS
   1 or 2 on one Game Boy; 1 or 2 players can also be linked in Match Play on two Game Boy units with the Video Link cable.

GAME BOY 1
   Used for 1-player and 2-player (alternating) games.

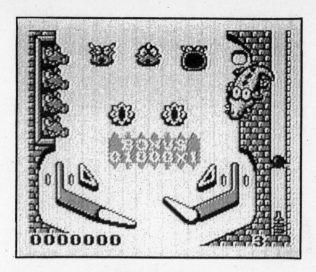

Winning a bonus.

GAME BOY 2

When connected with a Video Link cable, two players can engage in a simultaneous Match Play game.

CONTROL PAD

Arrow Pad: Press to make the Left flipper move.

"A" or "B" BUTTON: To start a round of the game, press and hold this button down until the onscreen plunger spring is fully retracted and then release the button to put the ball in play.

In game play, press the **A or B button** to make the Right flipper move.

PAUSE

Press the **Start** button to pause the game during play.

TYPE OF GAMES

From the opening screen, you can select from the following:

'Gator 1 Player. Single-player game.

'Gator 2 Player. For two players taking turns.

Matchplay A. Two-player simultaneous game using two Game Boys, Beginner Mode.

Matchplay B. Two-player simultaneous game using two Game Boys, Expert Mode.

NUMBER OF WORLDS:

There are 8 playing areas, including bonus stages. You will begin the game in the Shooter Lane (the starting plunger) which is alongside Screen D; the ball will travel up the right side of that screen and exit at the top of Screen C.

Here are the eight screens:

Screen A. Look for the fish in the upper left and right corners. Hit one with your ball and they'll become 'Gator Bait. Each fish the 'Gator eats makes him grow a little larger; when he is fully grown, he will be released from his cage and drop down the screen. Hit the 'Gator while he drops to earn a free ball or an increase in the Bonus Multiplier for points.

(You can only earn one free ball in each game. After you have gotten your freebie, each subsequent time you hit the falling 'Gator you will increase your Bonus Multiplier by 1.)

If you can knock out all three of the drop targets at the upper left corner of the screen, you will see new side savers and a saver post. Put the ball into the slot in the upper left corner to warp to Bonus Stage 3.

Screen B. You'll recognize this screen by the three 'Gators that are sitting in the middle. When they have reached their largest size, the side savers and saver post will appear; when the 'Gators have shrunk so that they disappear from the screen, the saves will also be gone.

What you want to do here is knock out the blocks and the drop targets on the left side of the screen here and then put the ball into the slot that opens there. This will warp you right into Bonus Stage 2.

Or, you could knock out all of the targets on the right side to open up the lane to Screen A.

There is also a special **Roll-Over Switch** in this screen: hit all three 'Gators at the same time when they are at their largest size. You'll pick up 100 extra points and a saver to help you make it into Screen A.

Screen C. This is the screen your ball is released into when you first start the game.

Try to hit all three of the little blocks on the left side of the screen. When you do, the lane that leads over to Screen B will open.

When all 4 of the Hearts at the top of the screen have been hit and lit, the side savers and saver post will appear.

Watch for when 8 dots around the lamp in the center start to flash on and off; hit the bumpers while they do to earn the highest points.

Shoot the ball through the **Loop Lane** on the right side of the screen to start the **Slot Machine** spinning. If all three of the Slots stop on a Star, the Bonus Multiplier will increase by one; if the Slots stop on a Fish, all of the post savers and side savers will appear. The booby prize—all of the savers will disappear and the Bonus Multiplier is reset to 1—happens if the slots stop on the third symbol which, for some reason, is an eggplant. Think of it this way: it's not a Star or a Fish.

Screen D. This is the screen you see before you start the game. The bottom of the plunger lane is at the right side. There are three 'Gators across the top of the screen and four 'Gator noses along the left side.

If you can shoot your ball directly into the Leftmost 'Gator's mouth, you will warp directly to screen C. Shoot the ball into the Center 'Gator's mouth and you'll go into Bonus Stage 1. Shoot the ball into the Rightmost 'Gator's mouth and you're back to the Shooter Lane.

If you can hit all of the 'Gator noses along the side, the side savers and saver post will appear. Flatten them again, and the 'Gator mouths at the top of the screen will reopen.

Bonus Stage 1. Knock out all of the blocks and then hit the 'Gator as he drops for 10,000 points.

Bonus Stage 2. Break the eggs, then hit each of the cute little baby 'Gators as they hatch for 30,000 points.

Bonus Stage 3. Hit each 'Gator as he sticks his head from the hole for 50,000 points.

'Gator Screen. Gulp. Bye-bye.

NUMBER OF LEVELS

There is just one level of play in the single Game Boy mode; if you connect two Game Boys with the Video Link cable you can play at **Beginner** or **Expert** level.

NUMBER OF LIVES

You start the game with 3 balls, but can earn one free ball per game by hitting the 'Gator in Screen A as described above.

SCORING POINTS

There are lots of points to be had in this game, including extra bonuses at the end of rounds that are determined by the Bonus Multiplier level you have achieved. Here are some of the points for various elements of the game:

Gator Mouths	1,000 points
Gator Noses	300 points

The gator swallows a wayward ball.

Kickers	10 points
Lanes	100 points
Holes	1,000 points
Bumpers	500 points.
Out Lane	500 points.

MATCH PLAY

The **Match Play** game is an entirely different sort of competition and a lot of fun. First of all, let us emphasize that you will need the following:

1. Two Game Boy machines
2. Two copies of the Revenge of the 'Gator game pak
3. A Video Link cable connecting the two Game Boys

To start the game, make sure the Video Link is plugged into both machines and the game pak installed in each. Then turn on both machines at the same time—this is an essential step, since otherwise the game play on both screens will not match.

From the opening screen, select Match Play A for the beginner level or Match Play B for the expert level.

You will see on screen a split pinball board. On each Game Boy, the holder's flippers will be on the bottom of the screen and the opponent's on the top half. Hitting the targets on your side will give you points;

hitting the targets on your opponent's side will lower his score. If you lose the ball on your side, you will lose 100 points.

There are three 'Gators near the flippers on each side. As the ball rolls over each, they will grow larger, then disappear and finally reappear. If you can time it so that there are three large 'Gators on screen at the same time, the saver post and side savers will appear. If your timing is such that all three 'Gators disappear at the same time, the savers will also disappear.

There are a number of special items in the Match Play game that are available to either player. *The winner of the special item is determined by which way the ball is travelling when the item is hit.* Here are the rewards or penalties for each item:

Number. You will win the number of points shown.

Heavy. Hit the letter "G" and the ball will become heavy.

Gravity. Hit the circle with the Up Arrow in it to increase the effects of Gravity on the ball.

Flipper. Hit the letter "F" and one of the flippers will disappear.

Center. Hit the circle with two blocks in it to make Center Blocks appear on screen.

Return. Hit the "R" for a return to the original settings for the game.

Savers. Hit the "S" for a full set of Savers.

Reverse. This is a particularly perverse one: hit the three little critters to reverse the scores of the two Video Link-ed players!

The game is almost over when either player's score reaches zero. You'll see the special "'Gator and Crossbones" symbol on the screen at that point; when the ball passes over this symbol the game is over. But until then, keep on playing—there are a few more surprises in store.

I ALWAYS WANTED TO KNOW

Why is there an eggplant in the slot machine? A very good question, and one that we would welcome some student of Japanese culture to explain to we American consumers. It seems that the eggplant is considered bad luck, kind of like poison ivy.

POWER PLAYER HINTS

When the ball disappears into one of the power-loaded holes just below a set of flippers, or if the ball is approaching the underside of a set of flippers, try pressing one or both buttons to raise the flippers. The ball just may pass through to an upper level in this way.

Don't be too hasty to swing at an approaching ball. Sometimes the best way to maintain control over a ball is to let it gently settle onto the flipper. Swing the flipper when the ball is at its top to push the ball relatively slowly to the same side as the flipper; swing the flipper when the ball is at its bottom to drive the ball across the screen at an angle.

Revenge of the 'Gator—Super Pinball is a trademark of Hal Laboratory Inc. @1989 Hal Laboratory Inc.

Skate or Die: Bad 'n Rad

AGE: 6 years-Adult
DIFFICULTY:Apprentice-Master of the Game

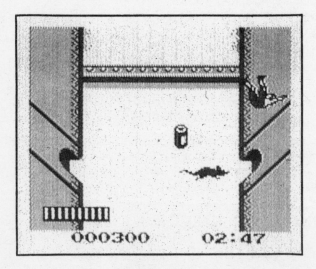

Yipes! A rat!

Given the choice, we'd rather skate. Even if we do have to overcome some rather difficult obstacles and fight against some rather nasty characters in this unusual combination of skateboarding skills and urban guerilla warfare.

Skate or Die on the Game Boy is, of course, based on the Nintendo Entertainment System hit, which was itself a version of the arcade classic. But the Game Boy version is very different, packing a great deal of arcade-like action into the tiny game pak and screen.

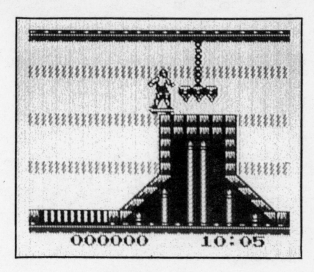

Waiting patiently.

This is an extremely well-crafted Game Boy offering. There is a great deal of detail in the screen images, and the response of the skater is quite good.

The story line is very simple: you have to get from the beginning to the end. Yes, there is a kidnapped girlfriend in there somewhere, but she is not much of a factor here. The fun comes from the challenge of scooting through the mountain passes, boardwalk, culvert, sewers and other exotic locales.

We worked with a very early version of the game, before it was completed for the American market.

MANUFACTURER: Ultra Software / (708) 215-5111

NUMBER OF PLAYERS: 1

CHARACTERS
In the early version of the game we examined, you play the role of "Joe," out to rescue your girlfriend "Carsa" from "Evil One," the enemy big boss.

CONTROL PAD
Arrows: Move your skater up, down, left or right within the Law of Gravity. You cannot merely drive up the side of a hill or tube, but must instead build up the speed to approach it properly.

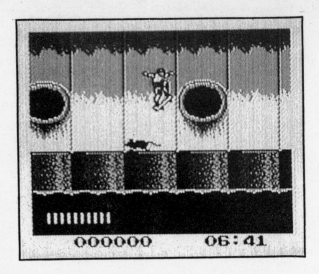

Down in the sewers.

"A" BUTTON: Makes your skater jump off his skateboard. Both he and
the board will continue to move in the direction he had been travelling,
and he will land on the skateboard to continue his adventure.

"B" BUTTON: Makes your skater squat down. Use this to avoid overhead obstacles, and also to build up speed as you climb up the sides
of tubes and hills.

PAUSE

To pause the game, press the **Start** button; to resume play, press the
button again.

RESET

Press the **A and B buttons** together with the Start and Select buttons to
reset the game.

NUMBER OF WORLDS

There are seven wild and wacky stages in this game. The game allows
you to choose the starting level each time you begin. Here are the stages:

1st Stage: Street. A left to right horizontal scroll. Watch out for trash
cans, falling flowerpots, fire hydrants, runaway tires and sudden
dropoffs. Be sure to duck under the overhangs and be ready to fight

against the nasty skateboarder at the end of the level who throws dangerous things at your head.

2nd Stage: By the Sea. A seaside pipe and breakwater, heading down the screen from top to bottom, just made for cruising on your skateboard. But be sure to watch out for tumbling barrels, spiked barriers and the pounding surf. You'll have to jump over a groove about a third of the way into the stage; soon afterwards you'll come to a bridge. Watch out! There's a sniper on the span. And there's a second sniper on the second bridge you come to.

3rd Stage. Down in the Sewer. What a mess. There are all sorts of nasty things down here—some of them we don't even want to know about. You start your journey with a climb up a few terraces, and then you are off on a race to avoid rats tumbling out of pipes, alligators (!) nipping at your heels and some very ugly and nasty things with snapping tails. Watch out for the low overhanging grates; be sure to duck down to avoid being knocked off your feet. As if that's not enough, there are also men tooling along in pontoon boats in the river of sewage; they'll poke at you with harpoons from underneath. Later on there are opponents with boomerangs. If you are caught—or miss a jump—you'll fall right into the YUCH.

4th Stage. In the culvert. You've got just a few minutes to make your way down this pipe, avoiding construction barricades, rats running from side to side and other strange obstacles. Be sure to ride up high on one side or the other of the pipe; remember that sooner or later the force of gravity will bring you back down into the center. There are also a few hidden traps right where you'd want to come back down. The further you go into the stage, the more pieces of abandoned drain pipe you will find blocking your way; if that's not enough, near the end of the stage there are several thin nets spread across parts of the culvert. Your final challenge is a jumping ramp: you'll have to go up at just the right moment, and then land in just the right place in order to duck down to scoot under one last bridge that passes overhead. Whew!

5th Stage. Mountain Path. Oooh . . . treacherous spikes to the right, a dizzying mountain valley to your left and lots of rocks and debris in the middle. There are a few skittish rabbits who have the unfortunate habit of running in front of your board, too. Sounds like our favorite ski run. But our favorite part of this game is the huge bird of prey circling overhead. It will swoop on down, if you are not careful, and pluck you off of the safety (?) of your skateboard and fly away with you to its nest. What a way to go!

6th Stage. Zooming Down to the Secret Training Room. This is a breathless downhill plunge from left to right. The new challenge here comes from a series of candles and blow torches above you and below you. You can jump over some, but we haven't figured out a foolproof way to get by them without getting at least a little bit singed. We recommend you just press on as fast as you can and try to outrun the flames.

7th Stage. The Secret Training Room. This stage is at the same time very slow and deliberate as well as extremely treacherous. You'll start at the base of a concrete tube; roll left to climb up the side and build up some speed and then zoom up the right side—pressing the **B button** at just the right moment to give you enough power to get over the lip. But don't go too far or too fast, or you will be squashed by a descending crusher. And once you're past that, and just starting to relax, watch out for the horizontal drilling bars that will come at you from the right. Oh yes: here is where the Big Boss is waiting, too!

NUMBER OF LIVES
You are given three lives at the start of the game.

TIMING
Each of the levels of the game has a different time allowance for completion:

Stage 1:	5 minutes
Stage 2:	3 minutes
Stage 3:	7 minutes
Stage 4:	3 minutes
Stage 5:	4 minutes
Stage 6:	7 minutes
Stage 7:	12 minutes

POWER PLAYER HINTS
In Stage 2, use the full width of the screen as much as you can to avoid the rolling barrels and other obstacles. Learn the rhythm of the incoming waves on the right side of the screen and scoot down to the waterside whenever you can, going back to the boardwalk as the waves come in.

SolarStriker

AGE: 6 years to Adult
DIFFFICULTY: Apprentice-Master of the Game

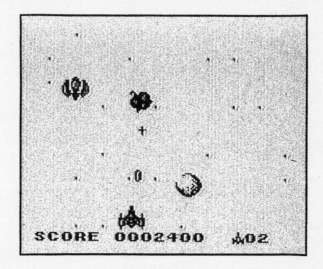

Is this all there is?

Yipes! We're under surprise attack by the forces of the planet Reticulon.

Well, all right, it's not really a surprise. They did give a couple hundred years of advance notice, but that was not enough time. The Reticulons have overpowered the Earth Federation Government.

But there is just one last chance: the Federation Army has somehow managed to hide a base on the moon, and there have developed a super fighter ship called SolarStriker. From the moon, the Federation is set to launch a mission to the home base on Reticulon and there destroy the main computer of the aliens.

Does all this sound familiar? Well, it looks familiar, too. SolarStriker is a rather unexceptional outer space shoot-em-up.

MANUFACTURER: Nintendo

NUMBER OF PLAYERS: 1.

CHARACTERS: You are the pilot of SolarStriker.

CONTROL PAD
Arrows: Move the ship Up, Down, Left, Right or on the diagonal.
"A" or "B" BUTTONS: Fires missiles. Keep the button held down for
rapid fire.

PAUSE   Press the Start button to pause the game; press the button again
to resume play.

RESET   To reset the game, press the A, B, Start and Select buttons at the
same time. The top score will remain in memory.

NUMBER OF LEVELS   There are six stages en route to the Reticulon
base. Each stage includes at least one boss who must be destroyed in order
to progress to the next challenge:

Stage 1: Stellar Area. The boss here is Epikhan, which will move left
and right at random, while firing. Worth 5,000 points.

Stage 2: Ozone. The boss is Destructor, a fighter ship that shoots bubble
bombs. Knock them down for 100 points each and destroy Destructor
itself for 5,000 more.

Stage 3: City. The boss is Ultra Crusher, which attacks with laser beams.
Worth 5,000 points.

Stage 4: Death Valley. The Sub Boss here is Omniquad, a four-part
challenge with a central computer. Each piece is worth 2,000 points
for a total of 10,000. The Big Boss is a mystery worth another 10,000
big ones.

Stage 5: Outer Base. You'll meet a four- part Sub Boss here by the name
of Xenocrypt. Each piece is worth 3,000 points, or 12,000 for the
whole shebang. The unnamed Boss is worth another 10,000.

Stage 6: Core of Base. The Sub Boss here is Quasi Obliterator, made
up of two moving parts, each worth 10,000 points. And then you get
to the Boss of Bosses for 20,000 more and a day's rest.

NUMBER OF LIVES
You will earn an extra SolarStriker for every 50,000 points you score.

SCORING POINTS

The Reticulon Army is made up of some 20 different types of attackers. Each are worth from 200 to 1000 points. We found it hard to distinguish most of the lesser enemies from each another.

Watch for the Anthrop (500 points). This bug-like guy fires large missiles; shoot down one of the missiles for an extra 500 points. You will also earn 200 points for each Power- Up you grab. Each Power-Up you take after your missiles are at their maximum level is worth 1,000 points.

The Terra Cannon blocks the roads in Stage 3. It is worth 1,000 points if you can dispatch it.

SECRET WEAPONS

The power of your missiles will increase each time you fly over one of the power-up items in the game. There are four power levels:

Single Shot. Basic power.
Double Shot. Yours after you grab your first power-up capsule.
Triple Shot. Grab two more power-ups.
Turbo Missiles. Yours after the fifth power-up.

Missile power will decrease by one level each time you are shot down.

SolarStriker is a trademark of Nintendo of America Inc. © 1990 Nintendo of America Inc.

Space Invaders
AGE: 6 years-Adult
DIFFICULTY: Novice-Hot Dog

It all started here. One of the very first video games, in arcades and crude home video versions, was Space Invaders. You were in control of a gun that moved left or right at the bottom of the screen, firing projectiles at an ever-faster, ever-closer squad of aliens dropping bombs. Each time the rows of aliens moved all the way to the left or right of the screen, they would descend one row.

It was a strangely addictive game, starting out relatively easy and becoming more and more frenetic in later stages.

Now, Space Invaders is back, in what may be its most comfortable and addictive format: the handheld Game Boy. Game play is virtually un-

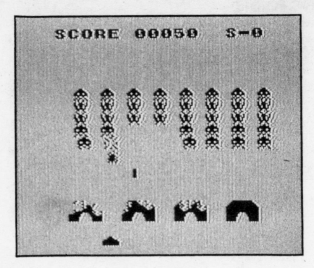

Shoot them aliens.

changed, with the addition of a version that allows head-to-head competition between two Game Boys connected with the Video Link cable.

You'll find the game a lot of fun; it's not the most sophisticated of computer games, but it does seem to merge right in with your brain waves.

MANUFACTURER: Taito America / (604) 984-3040

NUMBER OF PLAYERS
1 player, or 2 players connected by a Video Link cable (requires two copies of the Space Invaders game cartridge.)

CHARACTERS
It's you, defending the Earth, all by yourself.

CONTROL PAD
Arrows: Move the Laser Cannon Left or Right.
"A" or "B" BUTTONS: Fires Laser.

PAUSE
Press the Start button to pause the game; press the button again to resume play.

NUMBER OF LEVELS

The one-player game has 50 levels, if you can believe it!

NUMBER OF LIVES

In the one-player version of the game, you start with three laser cannons, losing each time one is hit by a bomb dropped by one of the descending invaders.

You will be awarded an additional laser cannon every 1,500 points.

SCORING POINTS

There are three types of descending invaders, plus a few mystery Flying Saucers that cruise across the top of the screen. You will score the following points for good shooting:

Invaders 3rd Class	10 points
Invaders 2nd Class	20 points
Invaders 1st Class	30 points
Flying Saucers	Mystery

TWO-PLAYER GAME

To play the head-the-head version, you'll need two copies of the Space Invaders game and a Video Link cable.

Both Game Boy units must be connected and turned on before the 2-player game is selected.

Choose the 2-player version and then press Start to enter the two-player mode. Then press the Select button to choose how many laser cannons each side will have, from 1 weapon, 3 weapons or 5 weapons.

In the 2-player game, each side controls a flying saucer that appears at the top of the opponent's screen. Moving the laser cannon on your Game Boy moves the saucer. Press the **A or B Button** to fire the laser cannon and the flying saucer at the same time.

Shooting a row or column of five invaders will cause them to appear on your opponent's screen.

To win the 2-player game:

- Complete five consecutive rounds, or
- Destroy your opponent's flying saucers, or
- Be alive when the invaders reach the bottom of your opponent's game screen.

Space Invaders is a registered trademark of Taito America Corp. © 1990 Taito America Corp.

Super Marioland

AGE: 6-Adult
DIFFICULTY: Apprentice-Hot Dog

An early underground treasure trove.

Mario is back, in an all-new adventure on the little screen of the Game Boy.

Many Nintendo game fans were disappointed to find that the NES game Super Mario Bros. 2 was *not* a true sequel to the original adventures of Mario and Luigi. It seemed like (in fact, it was) an adaptation of a completely different game that included familiar characters.

But worry no more: Super Marioland picks up where the first story left off. Our hero Mario (Luigi seems to have overslept) is off on an adventure in the once-peaceful world of Sarasaland. It's a world that includes a warped view of Egypt, with Pyramids, Sphinxes and other ancient oddities.

According to the story, the skies over Sarasaland were one day suddenly obscured by a huge black cloud. Breaking through the clouds was Tatanga, a mysterious space monster who has hypnotized all of the residents of the Sarasaland. Tatanga drives the war robot Pagosu, and shoots nasty rockets.

His next goal: to marry Princess Daisy and make her his queen as he rules over his captured land. In the meantime, he holds Daisy captive in the Chai Kingdom, the last of four worlds.

(Oh these little princesses. There seems to be an unending supply of them. Why do they always get themselves into these awful jams. What if Mario wasn't around? What if he was busy somewhere else?)

So Mario, freelance princess rescuer, sets off for Chai. He walks; he runs; he jumps; he bumps with his head; he throws superballs; he flies an airplane, and he pilots a submarine. We have Mario, Super Mario, Superball Mario and Invincible Mario.

The four kingdoms of Sarasaland are Birabuto, Muda, Easton and Chai. Each kingdom has four areas, with the boss of each kingdom in the third area. Areas 3 in worlds 2 and 4 are automatic-scroll shooting areas.

At the end of worlds 2 and 4 Mario goes undersea in his submarine and then airborne for a bit of shoot-em-up.

The game play is surprisingly good on the little handheld Game Boy device. If we were giving out a report card here, we'd award:

A for game action.

C for graphics, for a half-hearted use of the limited Game Boy screen

A+ for music and sound effects. The soundtrack to this game is a stunner when played through the Game Boy's stereo headphones and an absolute knockout if you patch it through your home stereo system and speakers. Music includes Egyptian-like themes, a bouncy version of Offenbach's Gaiety Parisien (also known as the "Can-can" song) and a new Mario theme. And just wait until you hear the zizzing and snagging of the monsters in stereo.

The History of Mario and His Brothers

This Game Boy adventure, as we have noted, is the third in a series of American versions of the saga of Mario and Luigi. Here's a little of what we know about their history thus far:

Super Mario Bros.

This is where it all began.

Once upon a time, the kingdom of the peaceful Mushroom People was invaded by the Koopa turtle tribe. Now these are not your ordinary turtles:

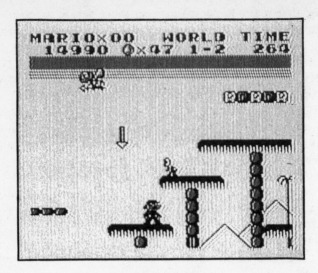

Watch out for the deadly arrows.

they had all sorts of magic spells and powers. Just to be mean, these troublesome turtles turn the good Mushroom People into stones, bricks and plants! (And they don't eat pizza, either.)

The good news is that the Mushroom King's daughter, Princess Toadstool, holds the power to undo the evil spell. The bad news is that Princess Toadstool is held captive by Bowser, the King of the Koopas. Mario and Luigi, those happy-go-lucky guys, hear the story of the unfortunate Mushroom People and set out to rescue the Princess.

The goal of the game is to make it to the final castle and rescue the Princess; the game also records points as you go along.

Super Mario Bros. 2

You remember our friend Mario? Well, he's retired from his exhausting effort to rescue Princess Toadstool in the Mushroom Kingdom. He's taking a nap one day, and he has the strangest dream: Subcon, the land of dreams, has been cursed by the evil Wart, and is completely under his spell. Mario hears a voice calling on him to rescue the people of Subcon.

A bolt of lightning flashes, and Mario awakes in his own little bed. He calls on his brother Luigi and his friends Toad and Princess and tells them about the dream. Together they go to a mountain for a picnic. There they find a small cave. Inside they discover a great stairway leading upwards. It is just like the one in Mario's dream, and when they go to the top of the stairs and open the door, together they find the world of Subcon!

Like Super Mario Bros., this is a moving challenge game. But rooms stretch out left and right and up and down from the starting point. There are underground rooms, called Sub-spaces, throughout the worlds. There are vines and chains to be climbed, too.

Unlike Super Mario Bros., the sequel game does not count points or include a timer. Instead, your goal is to progress all the way through the worlds and their various levels, defeating enemies, until you arrive at the final level.

In fact, Super Mario Bros. 2 is not strictly a sequel. Although the boys are back, their powers and the game action are different. This is more of an adventure game than an arcade action game. It is actually an adaptation of the Japanese Nintendo game called "Dream Factory."

Super Mario Bros. 3

Mario. Mario! Mario!!

This is the true successor to Super Mario Bros., with a touch of some of the fanciful elements of the Super Marioland Game Boy challenge mixed in.

There are all sorts of exciting new challenges in the game, including Winged Goombas, Giant Koopas and upside-down pipes. Mario himself adds a new shape to his repertoire: Racoon Mario. When he hits certain of the ? blocks in the game, they release a pair of fluttering wings; when Mario grabs a pair, he picks up a raccoon tail. He can now fly, and equally important, he can crush blocks by swinging his behind. Another new skill is the ability to swim.

This is also among the few Nintendo games where you can travel backwards through worlds you have already conquered. This is something that has some real value; for example, we found one situation where there were a set of blocks we could not destroy, but later on in the same world we obtained our racoon tail and then went to the left and back to the tough blocks to smash them and reveal their treasures.

The story line? Well, we think you might have guessed: Mario has to rescue the Princess. There are eight worlds, and the Koopas have cast spells on the kings of each and turned them into fearsome insects and animals. That's Mario's mission, and he must accomplish it by finding the magic wand that holds the spell.

The worlds are Grass Land, Desert Hill, Ocean Side, Big Island, The Sky, Ice Land, Pipe Maze and the Kuppa Castle. Our boy has to deal with giant

To the pyramids!

Mario-eating fish, gigantic turtles and a bad-dream version of the underground pipes of the first Super Mario Bros. game.

There are many bonus rounds, including card games, treasure rooms and a face-matching slot machine.

MANUFACTURER: Nintendo

NUMBER OF PLAYERS: 1.

VIDEO LINK: No.

CHARACTERS

Mario! Oh yes, there is Princess Daisy, held captive by Tatanga, and dozens and dozens of weird creatures that will stand in your way as you attempt a rescue.

CONTROL PAD

Arrows: Move Left or Right. The down arrow makes Super Mario squat down.

"A" BUTTON: Makes Mario Jump. In shooting scenes, the **A button** fires missiles or torpedoes. In this game, Mario and Super Mario will both jump the same height; the amount of time you hold down the **A button** will determine the height of the jump.

"B" BUTTON: Makes Mario Run. If Mario has picked up a Super Flower, the **B button** throws Superballs. In shooting scenes, the **B button** can also be used to fire missiles or torpedoes. If you press down the **B button** to make Mario run and then press the **A button** to make him jump, he'll soar higher.

PAUSE

Press the **Start** button to pause the game; press the button again to resume.

RESET

There is no **Reset** button on the Game Boy, but the same effect can be accomplished by pressing the **A, B, Select and Start buttons** at the same time.

NUMBER OF WORLDS

4: Birabuto, Muda, Easton and Chai.

NUMBER OF LEVELS

Three in each world, with the boss living in the third level of each world.

NUMBER OF LIVES

You'll start with 3, which will not be enough. You can gain extra lives by picking up 1-Up Hearts, collecting 100 coins or by choosing the winning row in the bonus round.

You'll lose lives when Mario is touched by an enemy, falls into a hole in the ground or when time runs out.

TIMING

Each world is timed; an experienced player will have little trouble completing each level in the allotted time. When the timer (displayed in the upper right corner of the screen) reaches the point where there are just 100 ticks left, the background music will speed up to give you a not-very-subtle hint to move along quickly.

HOW TO DEFEAT THE BEASTIES

Jump on them from above; knock them off blocks from below; throw a Superball at them, fire a torpedo from the submarine or a missile from the airplane. Not all enemies can be defeated in the same way as others—you'll have to engage in some painful experimentation.

SCORING POINTS

There are many ways to earn points. Here are some of them:

Coins are worth 100 point each;
Blocks broken by Super Mario give you 50 points;

You'll earn extra points if you can jump on several enemies in a row, bing-bing-bing.

Time remaining at the end of each world is multiplied by 10 and added to the score.

BONUS ITEMS:

1-Up Heart. Worth an extra Mario.
Coin. Collect 100 of them for an extra Mario.
?. A surprise bonus each time.

POWER-UPS:

Super Mushroom. Changes Mario into Super Mario, able to break blocks with his hard head.
Flower. When Super Mario picks a flower, he becomes Superball Mario and gains the ability to throw Superballs when you press the **B button.**
Star. When Mario catches a star, he becomes Invincible Mario for a short while and cannot be harmed by an enemy.

Note: If Super Mario or Superball Mario are touched by an enemy, they turn back into plain old ordinary Mario.

SECRET WEAPONS

Sky Pop. When did Mario learn to fly? This airplane comes equipped with missiles.
Marine Pop. Under the seas goes Mario in his one-man submarine. Stocked with torpedoes.

ENEMIES

There's a whole crew of new bad guys for Mario to fight.

BOSSES:

King Totomesu. Not a nice kitty, this fire-spitting feline runs the Birabuto Kingdom, the first world. Don't pet him, or jump on him. Try five superballs in his face. **5,000 points.**

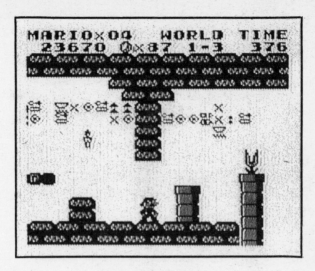

In ancient Egypt.

Dranonzamasu. A fire-breathing seahorse, this guy is the top honcho of the Muda Kingdom, protected by the indestructible Tamao. Shoot 20 torpedoes to sink him. **5,000 points.**

Hiyoihoi. A super Tokotoko stone statue, this guy is boss of the Easton Kingdom. He throws Ganchan rocks at Mario. Duck the rocks and throw 10 superballs at him. **5,000 points.**

Blokinton. The shy guy of the Chai Kingdom, he hides inside of the clouds. You'll need at least 20 missiles to bring him down to earth. **5,000 points.**

Each of the bosses is surrounded by a group of fearsome followers. Here is a description of many of them, including the number of points you'll earn if you can defeat them:

Batadon. A flying stone statue that will try to land on Mario. **400 points.**

Bunbun. A buzzing bomber who drops arrows from the skies. **800 points.**

Chibibo. This little mushroom is more scared of you than you are of it. **100 points.**

Chicken. This is a thunderbird who works for Tatanga. Fricassee him with a missile. **400 points.**

Chikako (Glitter). You'll need 10 missile hits to get through the protective barrier around this floating, glittering box. **800 points.**

Fly. A bloodsucker, you can defeat it with a well-timed jump. **400 points.**

Ganchan. Nasty, dangerous rocks that will drop from the sky. There is no way Mario can defeat them, but if your timing is just right, he can catch a ride on one of them.

Gao. A Sphinx-like statue who spits fireballs. **800 points.**

Gira. A creature shaped like a missile, or is it a missile that acts like a creature. Whatever, it takes off from a launch pad and aims straight at Mario. If Mario can land on it in the pad, he can defeat it. **400 points.**

Gunion. A tough sea creature, if you manage to hit it with two torpedoes, it will split in two and attack again. **800 points.**

Honen. This was a fish before Tatanga had lunch. It will swim up from the bottom; superballs won't work. **100 points.**

Kumo. A creepy spidery guy who will try to jump on Mario's back. **400 points.**

Mekabon. A head-butting robot, but his head is his weak spot, too. Land on it hard. **400 points.**

Nokobon. A basic Mario world turtle, this one with a bomb on its back. You probably won't want to jump on one. **100 points.**

Nyololin. A sneaky snake of a guy who throws poison balls. **800 points.**

Pakkun Flower. A Mario-eating plant that grows inside of the pipes; it will stick its head up and grab at you if you're not quick enough. Don't jump on one. **100 points.**

Upside Down (Headstand) Pakkun. New to the Mario series, this Pakkun flower dives down from pipes that are over your head. And heads are what it likes to bite. **400 points.**

Pionpi. A flying Chinese ghost, you can't get rid of him by jumping on him. The only offense that will work is a well-aimed superball. **800 points.**

Pompon Flower. A cute little flower, it scatters poisonous pollen. **800 points.**

Roketon. An attack airplane flown by the soldiers who guard Tatanga, it will shoot cannonballs at Mario in the Sky Pop. A missile will bring it down. **400 points.**

Suu. A sneaky spider who will drop silently from the ceiling of the caves onto Mario's head if he's not careful. **400 points.**

Tamao. Dragonzamasu's protector, this strange being cannot be defeated.

Tokotoko. A stone statue that runs around underfoot. **400 points.**

Torion. Mario-eating fish that travel in packs of three. Each one will require a torpedo. **100 points.**

Yurarin. A servant of Dragonzamasu, boss of the Muda Kingdom, this baby seahorse is a scaredyfish. You'll need two torpedoes to dispatch him. **400 points.**

Yurarin Boo. Yurarin's big brother, it spits fireballs. Don't bother with superballs; they won't work. **400 points.**

I ALWAYS WANTED TO KNOW

Where are the underground treasure troves in this game? Well, you don't expect us to tell you where *every* one of them is, do you? Where's the fun in that? Here are a few from worlds 1 and 2:

World 1-1. Start your count of pipes with the one to your left as you start the game. The first underground can be found in Tube 3. The second underground in this world is in Tube 6, just on the other side of the second chasm.

World 1-3. There are a whole bunch of pipes at the start of this world, but you want the 9th one, which comes just before the first gap in the floor.

World 2-1. This one's easy: there are two undergrounds in this world, one in each of the only two tubes you'll find.

World 2-2. The only underground area in this world is beneath the first tube you come to, sitting on a set of blocks suspended over the ocean.

Thanks. You've shown me how to get underground. Now, how do I get up above to run across the roof and avoid all of the obstacles below. Boy are you lazy! Okay, we'll tell about one: it's in World 1-3. Right at the very start of that world, you've got to catch a ride on a hidden elevator. To call the elevator, you've got to bump into the secret blocks at the start of the world.

One last question: How do I get through World 2-3? The ground keeps moving out from underneath me. That's what you get for playing Super Marioland while you're jogging! Just kidding. In this world, the screen moves all by itself no matter what you're doing. The trick is to keep Mario in the middle of the screen as you progress.

I don't want to have to start this game over again at the beginning every time. Neither do we. There is a hidden select mode in the game, but you can't get at it when you first turn on the machine. In order to earn the right to select a starting level, you have to complete the entire Super Marioland game twice. When you've done that (easier said than done, we know) you'll see an extra set of numbers next to your score. Use the control pad to select the level and round you would like to zoom to for

Ah, but it's not over yet.

more practice. Then again, someone who is good enough to win this game twice in a row doesn't really need all that much practice anyway.

SUPER SECRET!

Don't bother trying to beat the Sphinx Boss at the end of Level 1-3; just jump over him.

HOW TO ADVANCE TO THE NEXT WORLD

After Mario beats the boss of each world, he can enter the next world by stepping on the switch in front of the gate to each area.

POWER PLAYER HINTS

Just as you would in the NES Mario games, your first goal should be to pick up a few extra lives as insurance.

In this game, there are quite a few bonus lives to be had right from the start in World 1-1.

For example, just after the first set of pyramids and just before the first chasm, you'll come to a vertical line of coins hanging alongside a suspended group of blocks. Jump up onto the intermediate block and launch Mario toward the fourth block from the left. You'll be rewarded with a 1-Up Heart—be sure to grab it before it runs off the screen. By the way, there's a mushroom in the very next scene at the upper block, just before the next series of pyramids.

At the end of every area in the game, you'll come to the exit or goal, with entrances at top and bottom.

For example, at the end of World 1-1, you can scoot through the bottom door for a quick exit (valuable if you're running out of time) but if you can, ride up the two sets of elevator platforms and get off at the top. You'll be rewarded with a free pass to the bonus screen where you can pick up one, two or three extra lives or a flower.

Superballs thrown at a wall or block will bounce right back, and this can be used to defeat certain enemies.

If you see one of your enemies on a block above you, try knocking him off by bouncing into the block from below.

When Mario comes to places in the game where there a lot of small holes, he can get across them without jumping if he runs fast. Use the Right Arrow and the **B button** as a speedup.

There are hidden coins and mushrooms almost everywhere. As you learn the game, get into the habit of jumping up into any empty space just to explore.

POWER ZOOMING

There is no automatic continue in this game, except for one free continuation granted once at 100,000 points. If you reach this level and your game is over, the title screen will appear and a **Continue** option will be displayed. Move the Mushroom using the **Select** button to Continue to pick up the game near where you ran out of lives.

Super Marioland is a trademark of Nintendo of America Inc. © 1989 Nintendo of America Inc.

·3·
The Puzzle Palace

Boxxle
AGE: 6 to Adult
DIFFICULTY: Apprentice-Hot Dog

The first puzzle.

Many years ago, one of the most popular handheld games used no batteries, microprocessors or LCD screens: it was a small pad of plastic or even wood that held a dozen or so movable tiles with numbers on them. There was one less tile than there were spaces on the grid: the goal was to slide these Chiclet-like tiles around until they were in the proper order.

With Boxxle, FCI has updated this slider game into a charming, fun, clever and challenging exercise for the brain that is perfectly suited for the

113

Game Boy. This electronic puzzler is likely to hook older children and adults who in past years have spent their time with Rubik's Cube. We also suspect, though, that many young players will appreciate its challenge too.

Apparently every Nintendo game needs a story, so here goes the official line from FCI: It seems there is this guy named Willy who has a job in a warehouse moving boxes around. He's doing this, we're told, to earn enough money to buy a wonderful present to win over the girl of his dreams.

How exciting can moving around boxes be? Well, you've got to move the boxes so that each one ends up sitting on the appropriate dot marked on the floor of the warehouse. There are walls in the way and twisty corridors to navigate. If you move the boxes into a corner or up against the wall, you may not be able to get behind them to push them into place. The trick here is to think through each screen and plan your moves carefully.

All along, Willy's work is accompanied by a bouncy sound track with a great beat. And Willy raises his arms in triumph and cheers when he succeeds—we suspect you will, too.

The game wisely includes a password feature, allowing you to re-enter the game at the highest stage you have cleared—otherwise this fun-filled game could lose its charm. And, the game even includes the option for the player to build three of his own warehouse scenes—a nice added feature that will allow you to challenge yourself and your friends with your own creations.

We looked at the Japanese version of the game, called Soko-Ban, as FCI readied the English-language adaptation for the American market. Soko-Ban, by the way, means Warehouseman in Japanese.

MANUFACTURER: FCI / (708) 968-0425.

NUMBER OF PLAYERS: 1.

CHARACTERS: You are Willy the warehouse worker.

CONTROL PAD
Arrows: Move Willy Up, Down, Left and Right. When Willy is *behind* a box, he can push it into place.
"A" BUTTON: Backs up one move if you make a mistake in the game. In the pregame menu mode, the **A button** executes your choice on menu screens.
"B" BUTTON: Cancels. Returns the screen to the previous menu.
Start: Calls up menu screens and also executes your choice from the menu.

NUMBER OF WORLDS: 108 screens of boxes.

PLAYING THE GAME

It's a lot harder than it looks. Use the arrow keys to move WIlly around the screen. He can push—he cannot pull—the boxes around. The goal is to place all of the boxes on the dots. When you have placed all of the boxes, you will move on to the next screen.

On the screen, you will see two sets of numbers in the upper right corner. The top number is the **Area** and **Screen Number.** Below that is a four-digit number that records the number of moves you have made in each warehouse. The number increases once for each square Willy moves—even when he is doubling back to get into position to move a box.

After each screen is cleared, you will see a menu with the option to go on to the **Next** screen, or to **Select** another one of the screens in the current area. Note that you cannot select a screen in a different area—you'll need to earn your way into another area, or enter it using a password from another session. On the same menu, you will see the **Passkey** for the game thus far.

If you choose to Select a different screen, you can use the arrow keys to step through a display of available screens. When you see the warehouse you want to clear, press the **A button** or the **Start** button.

BACKING OUT

If you manage to get one of the boxes blocked—and believe us, you will—you can redo your move by immediately pressing the **A button.** If you have made another move, even if Willy is pushing against a wall or box he cannot move, you will not be able to undo the move you want.

RETRY

If you become completely blocked and want to try again, press the **Start** button. To try the same screen again, select **Retry.** If you want to try another screen, choose **Select.**

If you choose Retry, the screen you just left will reappear. Press and hold the **A button** and the boxes will move in the same order you moved them in the previous game. When the screen has retraced your steps to the point where you want to resume, release the **A button** and start playing.

We just made a bad move.

BUILDING YOUR OWN WAREHOUSE

You can create as many as 3 warehouse screens per game; they will stay in the system's memory until the power is turned off.

Select **Create** from the menu screen. You can build your warehouse with small or large boxes; the larger boxes make for an easier game.

Select the boxes, walls and dots and place them on the screen using the arrow keys. Press the **A button** to lock them in place. Press the A **button** and one of the arrow keys to create a continuous line.

To erase a box, wall or dot, push the **B button** until the Erase Square is flashing, and then move it with the arrow key until it is at the location where you want to erase. Press the **A button** to execute the command.

When you finish drawing the map, move the cursor to where you want Willy to begin. Push the **Start** button to play the game you have created.

From within the create screen, choose **Select** and then use the arrow keys to step through as many as three of the screens you have created. When you are ready to play, press the **Start** button.

The manual includes a page of graph paper you can use to design your own Boxxle screen; you can buy graph paper or make your own with 17 boxes across and 17 boxes down.

SCORING POINTS

This game is not scored. Instead, you goal is to get as far into the 108 screens as you can.

I ALWAYS WANTED TO KNOW

I can't get the hang of this game. Can you step me through the opening screen so that I can get a feeling for how to play? We'd be glad to. Follow these instructions exactly to get an idea of the solution of No. 01-01. When we say RIGHT, that means move Willy one full box right.

RIGHT, RIGHT, DOWN, DOWN, DOWN, DOWN.

At this point, you have moved the top block into a position where you can get ready to move it through the narrow opening to the right side of the screen. Now, you need to get into position to push it to the right.
RIGHT, DOWN, DOWN, LEFT, LEFT, UP, RIGHT, DOWN, RIGHT, UP.

The box is now in position. We need to move Willy behind it and then position the box in the upper dot position so that it is out of the way for the other boxes.

LEFT, UP, RIGHT, RIGHT, RIGHT, DOWN, RIGHT, UP, UP.

Now, get Willy back to the other side and let's move the second box.

DOWN, LEFT, LEFT, LEFT, LEFT, UP, UP, UP, UP, LEFT, LEFT, DOWN, RIGHT.

Move the box over to the other side.

UP, RIGHT, DOWN, DOWN, DOWN, DOWN, RIGHT, DOWN, DOWN, LEFT, LEFT, UP, RIGHT, DOWN, RIGHT, UP, LEFT, UP, RIGHT, RIGHT, RIGHT, DOWN, RIGHT, UP.

Again, return Willy to the other side and retrieve the last block.

LEFT, LEFT, LEFT, LEFT, UP, UP, UP, LEFT, LEFT, DOWN, RIGHT, UP, RIGHT, DOWN, DOWN, DOWN, RIGHT, DOWN, DOWN, LEFT, LEFT, UP, RIGHT, DOWN, RIGHT, UP, LEFT, UP, RIGHT, RIGHT, RIGHT.

See! Wasn't that easy? In this first screen, you should get an idea for all of the movements you'll need. This particular solution—93 moves in all—is only one way to clear this screen, by the way.

USING PASSWORDS

At the end of each level of the game, you will see a four-character password. Write it down for later use to re-enter the game at this point.

To use the "Passkey" feature, select it from the opening screen. Use the arrow keys to move the cursor to the character you want to enter, and then press the **A button** to input it. To erase a character, use the **B button**. When the entire password has been entered, select END and then press the **A button.**

Dexterity

AGE: 8 years-Adult
DIFFICULTY: Apprentice-Hot Dog

This guy Dexter Doolittle has a wonderful imagination. Among the special places he can transport himself to is his "magic puzzle room." In this room he can turn things around, upside down even flip them over, like some huge jigsaw puzzle.

This challenge combines a jigsaw puzzle, a maze and a labyrinth. When a player changes all of the colors of the blocks to the opposite color, he or she clears a round. There are special items, magic puzzle friends and treats, special bonus and super bonus stages and other surprises hidden about.

A player who clears all of the rounds gets to challenge King Tojo at the end.

New players may want to leave the title screen untouched for about 10 seconds; the machine will shift into a demonstration of game play.

We took a look at a very early preproduction version of this game.

MANUFACTURER: SNK Corp. / (800) PLAY-SNK.

NUMBER OF PLAYERS
1, or 2 players with two copies of the game pak, a pair of Game Boys and the Video Link cable.

CHARACTERS
You are Dexter Doolittle, a guy with a great imagination.

CONTROL PAD
Arrows: Throws movable blocks.
"A" BUTTON: Flips a panel.

"B" BUTTON: Lifts up magic puzzle friends placed between the panels.
Select: Selects modes before the start of the game.

PAUSE

Press the Start button to pause the game; press the button again to resume play.

NUMBER OF LEVELS: 30.

SCORING POINTS

Ghost	100 points
Snowman	200 points
Jellyfish	100 points
Humphrey Owl	200 points
Bug Eye	100 points
Sweeps	200 points

SPECIAL ITEMS

Hammer. Stuns everything on the screen for three seconds.

Heart. Gives an extra life.

Hour Glass. Gives an extra 10 seconds of play.

Fruit Change (F). Changes enemies into bonus food.

Block Change (B). Changes enemies into movable blocks.

Scary Skull. Indicates the end of the bonus stage.

Bomb. Three seconds after it appears, it will explode and turn all tiles to white.

Trigger. Once this has exploded, tiles will only flip to a white field.

Maze (M). Takes player to the maze stage.

Key. Appears in the maze stage only; needed to go to regular game stage through locked door.

Door. Exit from maze stage to regular game.

Cherry. Adds 100 points.

Apple. Adds 200 points.

Peach. Adds 400 points.

Watermelon. Adds 800 points.

Ice Cream Cone. Adds 5,000 points.

Flipull

AGE: 8 years-Adult
DIFFICULTY: Apprentice-Master of the Game

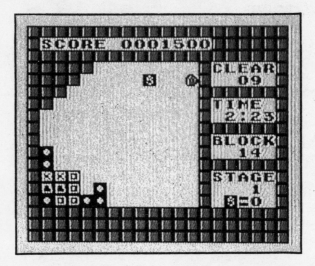

Flipull is "high impact aerobics for the brain."

This game is a cross between Chinese Checkers and Pinball.

The people at Taito call it "high-impact aerobics for the brain," and that's a pretty fair description. The goal is to knock out a pile of assorted cubes before time runs out; you do this by throwing a block across the screen and hitting a matching design. You can throw blocks directly, or you can bounce them off the walls. Matching blocks will be cleared out, and the next cube in the line will bounce back.

You'll use the arrow keys to move up and down the "ladder" on the right side to put your block in the correct position, and then **A or B button** to throw the block.

The game gets more and complicated and fast in the upper of the 50 levels in the one-player game; for a really "cube-ular" challenge, you can link two Game Boys with a Video Link cable for a head-to-head block-throwing contest.

In some of the upper levels of the game, special pipe obstacles will appear, stopping any blocks you throw across the screen. The only way to get blocks through the pipes is to bounce them off the ceiling and down through the top of the pipe, which is a lot easier to say than do.

You play the role of an unnamed, cute little guy who is trying to clear away troublesome blocks. That's it; no outer space aliens, no ancient curses, just a nice little game without a story line, at least in the preproduction version we worked with.

MANUFACTURER: Taito America / (604) 984-3040

NUMBER OF PLAYERS: 1, or 2 players using two Game Boys connected with a Video Link cable and two copies of the Flipull cartridge.

CHARACTERS: You are the Thrower of Blocks.

CONTROL PAD
Arrows: Move the block to be thrown up or down the "ladder" of positions along the right side of the screen.
"A" or "B" BUTTON: Throw Blocks

NUMBER OF LEVELS
There are 50 puzzle levels in the one-player game.

NUMBER OF LIVES
The current game is over when the timer reaches zero and you have not cleared the screen, or if you are blocked and cannot make a move.

SCORING POINTS

Clear 1 block.	100 points
Clear 2 blocks on one toss.	400 points
Clear 3 blocks on one toss.	900 points
Clear 4 blocks on one toss.	1,600 points
Clear 5 blocks on one toss.	3,200 points

Time bonus. 10 points for each second remaining on the clock.
Block bonus. 1,000 points for reaching goal, plus 1,000 points for each additional block you can hit until you have no more moves to make.

SPECIAL BLOCKS
When you remove five or more blocks at the same time, you will be rewarded with a Special block (a block with an "S" within). These blocks

Flipull Blocks

do not require a match to be removed. Each player will start the competition with three S blocks.

POWER PLAYER HINTS

Go for ricochet shots to remove more than one block at a time to score high points.

Treasure those Special blocks; they may be the only way to get out of some traps you'll find yourself in.

Pipes can be useful to bounce blocks off the ceiling.

POWER ZOOMING

You can continue your game three times. To continue, press the Start button when the Game Over screen appears. To end the game, press Select to choose the End option and then press the Start button.

TWO-PLAYER GAME

To use the two-player version of Flipull, you will need a pair of Game Boys, a Video Link cable and a pair of Flipull cartridges.

Game play is generally the same as the one-player competition. There is no time limit, and each player starts with two Special blocks.

If you clear two or more blocks at the same time, your opponent will receive those blocks minus one on his own screen.

If you clear a row or line of five blocks at the same time, a Special block will appear in the pile, but both players can try to get it.

If either player clears a line or row of blocks four times consecutively, a row of blocks will appear at the bottom of the opponent's pile.

There are several strategies to win a two-player game, including:

- Reducing the pile of blocks on your screen to reach the goal;
- Pushing your opponent's pile of blocks to the ceiling, or
- Leaving your opponent with a block he cannot use.

Flipull is a trademark of Taito America Corp. © 1990 Taito America Corp.

Ishido: The Way of Stones

AGE: 8 years-Adult
DIFFICULTY: Apprentice-Hot Dog

One of the most ancient of games has made it all the way to the most modern of toys with the arrival of Ishido for the Game Boy.

According to Nexoft, this game is based on a set of four related games that have mysteriously grown up in four unrelated cultures: the Chinese game called Shi tao, the ancient Celtic game called Runa futhark, the Mayan Indian game of Kami-a-hota and the Japanese game of Ishido.

Like any good puzzle game, this one is very easy to play and extremely difficult to master. The goal of the game is to place as many stones as possible in the grid. There are six different patterns and six different symbols for a total of 36 different design on a total of 72 stones; therefore there are two of each design. The screen is made up of 96 squares in 8 columns and 12 rows.

The game combines a bit of the luck of the draw with the brain of the player. There is a single-player game as well as a two-player version.

We looked at preproduction materials.

MANUFACTURER: Nexoft / (213) 540-4778

NUMBER OF PLAYERS: 1 or 2.

CHARACTERS: You are the placer of stones.

CONTROL PAD

Arrows: Moves the onscreen touchstone to indicate the location for the next stone.

"A" BUTTON: Places a stone; selects a command.

"B" BUTTON: Opens a menu; cancels a command.

PLAYING THE GAME

The touchstone is used to indicate where the next stone is to be placed. Place the stones on the board one by one until all 72 have been placed, or until no more stones can be placed.

There are four basic rules of Ishido stone placement:

Placing a stone next to a single stone. A stone can be placed next to a single stone only if the pattern or the symbol of the stones match.

Placing a stone next to two adjacent stones. The symbol of the stone being placed must match one of the adjacent stones, and the pattern must match the other stone.

Placing a stone next to three adjacent stones. The pattern must match at least one of the adjacent stones and the symbol must match the remaining stones.

Placing a stone in a location surrounded by four stones. The pattern must match two of the stones, and the symbol must match the remaining two. This pattern is called a "4-way."

SCORING POINTS

The final objective of Ishido is to score as many points as possible. Points are awarded as follows:

A stone adjacent to 1 stone.	1 point
A stone adjacent to 2 stones.	2 points
A stone adjacent to 3 stones.	4 points
A stone adjacent to 4 stones.	8 points

After a 4-way is achieved, all following points are doubled. Each successive 4-way doubles points again.

When the game is finished, additional bonus points are awarded based on the number of 4-ways achieved:

Single 4-way.	100 points
Two 4-ways.	200 points
Third 4-ways.	400 points
Fourth 4-way.	800 points

Bonus points continue to double for additional 4-ways.

THE SOLITAIRE GAME

It's you against yourself. The game continues until all stones have been placed on the grid, or until no more stones can be placed.

The designers suggest that new players concentrate at first on simply placing the stones. More experienced players can work to score as many 4-ways as possible.

THE CHALLENGE GAME

Two players take turns placing stones, competing for the highest score. The game continues until all stones are placed, or until no more stones can be placed.

Ishido is a trademark of Publishing International. © 1990 Nexoft Corporation; © 1990 ASCII Corporation; © 1989, 1990 Software Resources International.

Jeopardy!
AGE: 8 years-Adult
DIFFICULTY: Apprentice

Okay contestants, one more time, here's the question:

"One of television's longest-running and most thoughtful games, where contestants are given the answer and must come up with the question, packed it into a tiny Game Boy cartridge."

BUZZ!

"What is Jeopardy!?"

The Jeopardy! game is one of the more intellectual of television's game shows. Contestants select a category and a betting level (from $100 to $500 in the basic game and $200 to $1,000 in Double Jeopardy!). The answer is revealed, and then the first contestant to hit his buzzer gets the chance to ask the question that matches it.

We looked at an early preproduction version of the Game Boy cartridge. The following description is based on the NES version. The photos in this section, though, are from the Game Boy screen.

MANUFACTURER: GameTek / (305) 935-3995

NUMBER OF QUESTIONS

According to GameTek, there are hundreds of questions and answers in the Jeopardy! database in the game pak. The categories and questions

Let's meet today's contestants!

are randomly selected for each game; it is possible that repetition will occur. If you want to "reshuffle" the file, press the Reset button on the control deck to start a new game.

NUMBER OF LEVELS

There are three levels of difficulty, from 1 (Easiest) through 3 (Most Difficult.) The level is selected at the opening screen by Player 1.

You will start the game in plain old Jeopardy!, move on to Double Jeopardy! and end up in Final Jeopardy!

HOW TO PLAY JEOPARDY!:

Contestants are given 10 seconds to decide if they want to make a guess; once they have been recognized, they are allowed 40 seconds to enter the question using the on-screen cursor.

In the television game, the contestant would call out his question. In the Nintendo game version, the contestant who buzzes first enters into a screen with a typewriter-like character display. The player must move the on-screen cursor and select letters to spell out the question.

If your question is correct, you will be awarded the amount of money you have wagered; if your question is incorrect, that amount will be subtracted from your current winnings. The other players are then given an opportunity to bet they can come up with the question for the answer. (The loser in a particular round cannot try again.)

Hiccup!

Play continues until the board is completely cleared of answers.

Hidden under one of the 30 windows is the **Daily Double.** The player who selects that particular square automatically gets to try that question. If you have winnings, you will be allowed to wager any amount up to the amount you have won; if you have no winnings, you can choose any amount up to the maximum of the game you are now playing ($500 in Jeopardy!, and $1,000 in Double Jeopardy!) If you come up with the correct question, you will win the amount wagered; if your question is incorrect, you will lose an amount equal to your wager.

TIMING

Contestants are given 10 seconds to decide whether they want to attempt a guess. They then are given 40 seconds to enter their question; on longer questions, this can become a tight race against the on-screen clock.

DOUBLE JEOPARDY!

After the Jeopardy! board has been cleared, you will enter into the Double Jeopardy! competition, which is just like Jeopardy! except that the amount of money for the bets has been doubled.

There are two Daily Doubles hidden on the board.

The player with the lowest dollar winnings in Jeopardy! gets to start the Double Jeopardy! round.

FINAL JEOPARDY!

The ultimate competition in this game is Final Jeopardy! Admission to this round is limited to those players who have winnings; if you "owe" money to the bank, you'll have to sit on the sidelines and kibitz like most television viewers.

In Final Jeopardy, all players are given the opportunity to come up with the question to match a single answer. Before the question is displayed, though, each player must make a bet. The amount of the bet can range from 0 to all of the money won in the game thus far.

POWER PLAYER HINTS

First of all, be careful with your spelling. Although the game will accept many near-misses in spelling, it will also reject some reasonable guesses. For example, one of the answers we faced in a "Nuts to You" category was about a 1929 Marx Bros. Hit. We entered, "Coconuts" but lost the round because the program wanted "Cocoanuts." Also be careful to be precise and complete: we entered "Musketeers" to one answer, and lost a round because the game wanted the full "Three Musketeers."

Take care if the question includes a number. Use the numeric characters or spell out the number.

If the question calls for a pair of words or names, enter the most commonly seen order. For example, enter "Abbott and Costello" and not "Costello and Abbott."

If the question is posed in the plural ("Who are," or "What are") be sure to enter a plural answer.

Spacing between words is optional (move the cursor to the spot between the & and the - and press **A or B buttons** to lock it in). If you are pressed for time, just ignore the spaces.

The biggest element of strategy in this game often comes in Final Jeopardy when you choose the amount of your bet. If you are behind, it probably is worthwhile to bet your whole stake (it's only play money, right?) and hope you will get the question correct and the leader will bet all of his money and guess incorrectly.

It is sometimes more complex if you are the leader. Let's say you have won $6,000 and your nearest rival has won only $2,750. In this case, it would be unnecessarily risky to bet more than $400. If you were to lose that amount, you would end up with $5,600. If the second place contestant was to bet all $2,750 and guess correctly, he would end up with $5,500 and still lose the game to you.

Kwirk

AGE: 8-Adult
DIFFICULTY:Apprentice-Master of the Game

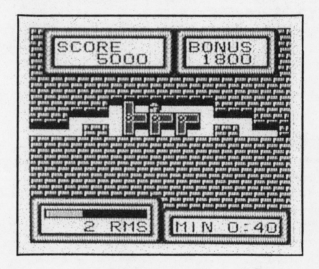

Turnstiles ahead.

Kwirk, the Chilled Tomato, is in a bit of a stew. Now seriously, folks, although we expect you may have a hard time believing this, we didn't make that one up: that is the opening line of the Kwirk maze and logic puzzler for the Game Boy. This is a very clever, engaging challenge that is perfectly suited for the handheld machine.

We'll get into the details of game play in a second. First, let's get back to the story line: "Kwirk and his girl, Tammy, were out painting the town tomato red, when they decided to check out this cool, subterranean labyrinth beneath the city's sizzling, hot streets. Well it seemed like a good idea at the time."

It seems that Tammy Tomato disappears, and poor Kwirk fears she has been kidnapped. Our hero sets out to solve a series of increasingly complex mazes, sometimes assisted by his vegetable buddies Curly Carrot, Eddie Eggplant and Pete the Pepper.

Kwirk makes his way across the mazes by turning giant turnstiles and moving small pebbles and huge blocks to clear passages and fill in holes.

There are three distinct games in the Kwirk cartridge. Going Up? and Heading Out? are available in single-player versions, and Heading Out? Vs. Mode is offered for tomato-to-tomato competition using the Video Link cable.

MANUFACTURER: Acclaim Entertainment / (516) 624-9300

NUMBER OF PLAYERS
1, or 2 with a pair of game paks, two Game Boys and the Video Link cable.

CHARACTERS
Kwirk and Tammy Tomato, with their vegetarian vanguard of Curly Carrot, Eddie Eggplant and Pete the Pepper.

CONTROL PAD
Arrows: Move Kwirk left, right, up or down.
"A" BUTTON: Starts the floor or room over.
"B" BUTTON: Not used during game play. During the selection process returns to a previous selection screen.
Select: Switches control to another vegetable when more than one is shown on screen.

GAME VARIATIONS
GOING UP?
The first game is Going Up?, which offers dozens of individual floors. You can choose where you want to start. There are three skill levels: Easy, Average and Hard and the user can then choose from floors 1 to 10 as a starting place.

The next option is a choice of Display Angles. Diagonal View shows the shadows of the blocks and walls, giving a 3-D perspective. Bird's Eye is shadowless, looking straight down from above. Game play is the same for both displays—pick the one that gives you a better feel for the challenge.

When you press the **A button,** you will be offered a choice of special control options:

REDO Gives you a quick return to beginning of the floor as an escape hatch when you have reached a point where you cannot possibly win.

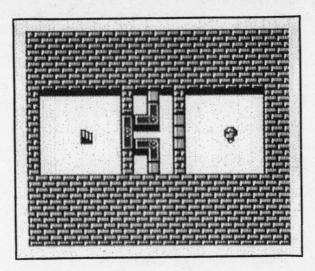

From here to there.

END Takes you back to the game selection screen.

BACK a move. The Game Boy retains the last 8 moves in memory and you can go through them one at a time.

There is no "score" in Going Up? other than the count of completed rooms. When a floor is completed, the game will give you a report on your accomplishments including the number of floors completed, the time required for the last floor and the number of steps taken to complete the round. Press Start to go on to the next room.

HEADING OUT?

The second game is Heading Out?, which presents a series of rooms connected by a continuous tunnel. In each of the three skill levels, there are 99 rooms to choose from. The floors appear in a different order each time you play the game. You can choose between the same two display options offered in Going Up?

Pressing the **A button** will remove Kwirk from a room and reset all of the obstacles to allow you to try over again.

The screen display of Heading Out includes a score that goes up with the completion of each room, plus a Bonus window; the faster a room is cleared the more bonus points are added to the score. Finally, the screen includes a clock of elapsed time as well as an indicator of the number of remaining rooms.

The top high scores of the current game session are displayed in the final window of the Heading Out? game. The scores are erased when the Game Boy is turned off.

To earn the highest possible score, solve the puzzle in the shortest period of time with the least total number of moves. You will start each puzzle with 2,000 bonus points that will be added to your score when a puzzle is cleared. Every 10 seconds, 100 points will be deducted from the available bonus.

VS. MODE

Here's your chance to pit your tomato against your friend's. Okay, so tomatoes don't have pits! Why not go stem-to-stem?

The key here is the use of the Game Boy's Video Link cable, *plus* a pair of Kwirk cartridges. Connect both units with the cable with the power turned off, insert the game pak in each machine and then turn on the power. The player who presses the Start button first will be in charge of making the initial selections.

Choose VS. MODE from the game selection menu and then select a Skill level from Easy, Average or Hard.

Then *each player* must select the Number of Rooms to be cleared. For an evenly matched competition, both players can choose the same number; to handicap the better player, he should be assigned more rooms to be cleared than his opponent.

Next, choose the type of tournament. Options include a 1-game challenge as well as Best of 3, Best of 5, Best of 7 and Best of 9 tournaments. In such a tournament, the first player to win a majority of the games will win: for example, in a Best of 7 series, the first player to win four games will be awarded the title.

The final selection is a choice of Display Angle.

To start over, press the **A button.**

During a VS. game, the onscreen display includes information on both your progress and that of your opponent. The first player to complete all of the rooms on a level will win the contest.

OBSTACLES

There are four basic types of obstacles to be found inside the mazes:

Brick Walls. These are solid walls that cannot be moved. Your only choice is to work your way around them.

Turnstiles. There are four types of these spinnable sets of blocks, available in single, double, triple or quadruple versions. The turnstiles can be turned around the central axis—marked with a circle—unless

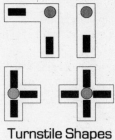

Turnstile Shapes
in Kwirk

there is a block or other obstacle in the way. If the turnstile is unable to turn, your challenge will be to move the block that is in the way.

Blocks. Blocks come in rectangular and square shapes and can be moved up, down, left or right to free blocked turnstiles, clear paths or fill in holes.

Holes. Kwirk cannot go over a hole in the maze. In order to get past one, then, you will have to fill it in with a block that matches the shape of the hole.

POWER PLAYER HINTS

Use the Veggie vanguard when you find them in a room. Many of the advanced puzzles cannot be solved without them.

To take control of a friendly vegetable, press the Select button until the vegetable you want to use is blinking. Then control him in the same way you have been moving Kwirk.

To switch control to another vegetable, press the Select button again.

To complete a room or floor, all of the available veggie friends must pass through the exit door or reach the stairs, depending on the game. If Kwirk or any of the veggies get caught, you'll have to try over again.

QBillion

AGE: 8-Adult
DIFFICULTY: Novice-Master of the Game

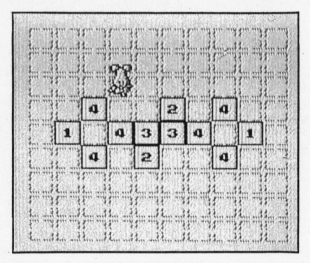

An easy "A" game.

Story? No story. Just a guy named Mr. Mouse who likes to move around blocks.

This is a very simple puzzle game, perfectly suited to the Game Boy. Did we say simple? The deeper we got into this game, the deeper were the furrows on our brows. Put one of these babies into your handheld computer when your plane is on the runway in Boston, settle back and when you look up again you'll be in Los Angeles. Or maybe plug in when the school bus arrives and . . .

There are six types of marathon mouse competitions, with a total of 120 predesigned screens. You can also play a head-to-head game against a friend using the Video Link cable. And, you can also design your own puzzle patterns to challenge yourself or an opponent.

There may be no story, by the way, but we do love the little dance of joy that Mr. Mouse does each time you help him to solve a puzzle. What a guy!

MANUFACTURER: Seta U.S.A. / 702 795-7996

NUMBER OF PLAYERS

1 or 2. Two players can engage in head-to-head competition using the Video Link cable (with a pair of game cartridges and Game Boy machines.)

CHARACTERS: You are Mr. Mouse, mover of blocks.

CONTROL PAD

Arrows: Move Mr. Mouse up, down, right or left. Also used to select menu items and select Tic-Tac-Toe squares.

"A" BUTTON: Pushes block. Selects shape to be erased. Positions blocks in Edit Mode.

"B" BUTTON: Undoes the last block move. Erases flashing shape of symbol blocks. Erases block under the cursor in Edit Mode.

Select: Restarts puzzle in Game A, and 2-player mode. Selects type of block to be placed in Edit Mode. Restarts puzzle in Game B.

NUMBER OF LEVELS

There are 120 patterns offered in the standard game. Players can also define their own puzzles using the game's Edit function.

GAME A

The basic game has no time limit and you can restart the puzzle using the Select button at any time with no penalty.

You will be able to select Slow, Normal or Fast movement for Mr. Mouse. Remember, this is not an arcade game: all you are changing here is the speed at which he responds to presses of the arrow key to move him around on the screen. We found the normal or slow settings to be most comfortable, but all three worked well.

The second choice from the menu screen allows you to select a starting level. If you select Game, you can next select any of the first 30 levels as a starting point. If you select Password, you can enter a password you've earned in a previous session. See Power Zooming for more details.

Once you're into the game, start moving those blocks. The key rule is this:

Mr. Mouse can only push a block that sits one level above the one he is standing on. For example, to move a block on level 4, our mouse must be standing on level 3; to move a block on level 3 he must be standing on level 2 and to move a block on level 2 he must be on level 1. He can also move a Level 1 block around on the screen.

To erase a symbol block, Mr. Mouse must arrange at least 4 blocks with the same number and symbol into one of 5 possible shapes. When you have created one of the shapes, the blocks will flash on and off on the screen. If you have brought together more than 4 blocks, you may have more than one shape to be erased; use the **A button** to select which of the shapes you want to erase. Press the **B button** to erase the selected shape; you can press the **B button** again to undo the last block move made by Mr. Mouse.

GAME B

It's you against the computer in a combined game of QBillion and Tic-Tac-Toe.

You'll play a series of puzzles, competing against the computer and the clock. The winner of each puzzle wins the selected Tic-Tac-Toe square.

The goal is to match groups of four blocks with the same shape. When they are matched, they will disappear from the screen. In this game, points are awarded for erasing shapes, and you must receive at least 50 points in order to win the square. Points are awarded as follows:

Four-block square.	5 points
Four-block vertical column.	3 points
Any other shape.	1 point

When the puzzle is solved, half of the time remaining on the timer will be added to your score.

The Tic-Tac-Toe competition is a best-of-five games, with each game a best-of-five set challenge. Does that sound confusing? Think of it this way: the first player (you or the computer) to win three sets wins a game and the first player to win three games wins the match.

You win a set, of course, by standard Tic-Tac-Toe rules. Your goal is to end up in possession of three squares in a row: up, down or diagonally.

2-PLAYER GAME

The head-to-head challenge under QBillion requires two Game Boys, each with its own QBillion game paks and the Video Link cable.

Contestants can compete in Game A or Game B, as described above, or in Game C, which is a combination of both. In all cases, you will be

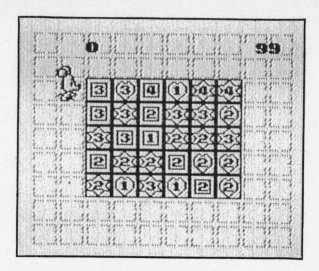

Your basic "B" game.

competing to fill in a Tic-Tac-Toe square. You can each try for the same square, in which case the first player to clear a screen wins the square; or, each contestant can race to clear a screen to win a different Tic-Tac-Toe square.

You can consult the status of the Tic-Tac-Toe board at any time by pressing the STart button.

Note that once a player enters a puzzle in the 2-player mode, he cannot leave without solving the puzzle or losing it.

EDITING YOUR OWN QBILLION PUZZLE

Select 1-Player and then Editor to create your own puzzle. You can make them for your own challenge, or you can set up a game where you and a friend take turns creating puzzles and solving each other's most difficult assignments.

Your options under Edit are:

Edit. To build new puzzles. Select the puzzle name to build and then use the **A button** to place the block in the location you want. Press the **Select** button to change the shape of the block to be place. Move the onscreen "hand" over a block you've already placed and press the **A button** again to add another level of block.

Game. To solve one of the problems you have built; as many as 16 puzzles can be created and held in memory. Games will be erased when the power is turned off.

Erase. Erases one of the puzzles created in the current session.

POWER PLAYER HINTS

Always look for ways to move blocks around into positions where they will be more valuable.

A four-block square made up of anything but 1s is a deadlock, and should be avoided.

POWER ZOOMING

When you solve the first 30 puzzle patterns of QBillion, you will be rewarded with a password that allows you to reenter the game with access to the next 10 puzzles. After you solve each group of 10, you will win the key to the next 10.

Passwords are four-letter words. Use the Up or Down arrows to scroll through the alphabet. Use the Right arrow to move on to the next letter of the word once the correct character is displayed; you can use the Left arrow to backspace to redo a mistake. Press the Start button to begin the game when the password has been properly entered.

To take a peek at puzzles 31 to 40, use this password:

WALL

QBillion is a trademark of Seta U.S.A., Inc. © 1990 Seta U.S.A., Inc.

Shanghai

AGE: 8 to Adult
DIFFICULTY: Apprentice-Master of the Game

This game has come a long, long way. Shanghai is a Japanese interpretation of the ancient Chinese game called Mah Chiang, which an American developer adapted for the U.S. market in the 1920s under the name of Mah Jongg.

Originally played with cards, then carved bamboo and finally ivory tiles, it can now be displayed on the state-of-the-art screen of the Nintendo Game Boy.

Watch the maiden's eyes.

This is a great game to play on a long airplane or car journey, or some other time when you are prepared to sit down and concentrate for a period of time. Shanghai will not get your heart pumping like a good game of pinball or a Mario adventure, but it will instead exercise your brain, and that's not a bad thing to do.

Mah Jongg dates back more than 2,500 years to the time of Confucius. It was said to have been invented by Chinese sailors to break the boredom of long ocean voyages. The game eventually made its way to Western players, with a worldwide Mah Jongg craze striking in the 1920s.

You are given 144 tiles, arranged in a shape sort of like that of a dragon. The center of the stack of tiles is five tiles deep, while the edges are only one tile deep. Your goal is to remove Free Tiles from the screen, one at a time or in matching pairs, until there are no more left on the screen.

Sound easy? Well, it is. But like checkers, chess and dominoes, the better you get at this game, the more difficult it becomes.

The game includes a nicely written and produced set of background musical numbers—the player is able to select among the three songs for a change of pace.

The American version includes both Chinese characters and an English version with letters, numbers and symbols.

Your view is from directly above the layout, which is vaguely in the shape of a dragon. The center section is stacked five tiles deep, with the tiles on the outer layer only one layer deep.

If you manage to clear the screen of all 144 tiles, a dragon will appear bearing a message of good fortune.

The Story of Mah-Jongg

Mah-Jongg was "invented" by an American, Joseph Babcock and patented in 1920. Babcock adapted some of the rules of Western card games, including rummy, to the features of the Chinese tile game. The U.S. experienced a Mah-Jongg craze in the 1920s.

Mah-Jongg consists of 144 tiles, 108 of which are suit tiles of bamboos, circles, and characters. Each suit has 36 tiles numbered 1 through 9, with 4 tiles of each numeral. There are also 28 honor tiles—4 each of the 4 winds, marked E, S, W, and N for the compass directions; and 4 each of the 3 dragons, red, green, and white. Finally, there are 8 bonus tiles, 4 each of flowers and seasons.

In the classic four-player game, each contestant begins with 13 tiles except the player designated "East," who has 14. The players draw from a square with walls that are 18 tiles long and 2 tiles high. Play opens with East discarding a tile and proceeds as each player, in turn, either takes a discarded tile or draws one from the wall. A player wins with a complete hand (woo) of four sets plus a pair.

A set of three tiles in one suit is a chow; three tiles of one suit and rank, or dragons, or winds make a pung. And a pung plus a fourth like tile makes a kong.

MANUFACTURER: Hal America / (503) 644-4117

NUMBER OF PLAYERS: 1.

CONTROL PAD
   Arrows: Used to move the onscreen "hand" that serves as a cursor.
   "A" BUTTON: Used to select a pair of tiles and remove them, and to enter selections from the subscreen menu.
   "B" BUTTON: Used to cancel selections, and to return the screen to its original state after options have been used.
   Start: Starts the game when pushed at the title screen.
   Select: Pressing Select during the game will display the Subscreen. Choices from the menu can be made by moving the arrows up or down. Press the **A button** to enter a choice; press the **B button** to cancel a selection.
      Available from the Subscreen are:

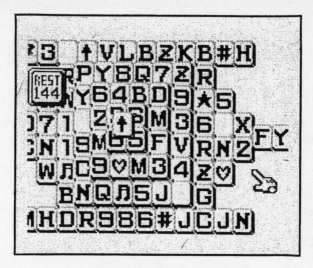

An English-language screen.

New Game. You can choose to enter the three-letter code for a particular dragon layout. The starting code is HAL; for a few other passwords, see the Secret Password section of this chapter.

Option. Three special facilities are available here:

>**Hint.** The computer will show you pairs of matching characters that can be chosen. Press the **A button** to scroll through possible hints; press the **B button** to cancel out of the hint screen to make your move.

>**Playback.** Allows you to take back a move already made. Each push of the **A button** will restore one pair of tiles to the Dragon.

>**Face.** Switches the characters from Chinese to English characters, numbers or symbols, using the same layout.

BGM. You can choose among three different musical selections for background music.

Start & Select: Pressing the Start and Select button together when the title screen appears moves you directly to a prompt for the Name of a particular dragon layout. Enter the three-letter password using the arrow keys.

NUMBER OF WORLDS

The layout of the tiles can be changed by going into the subscreen and choosing a new design. In addition, each time the tiles are laid out on the screen the distribution of tiles is different, and a new game can be selected at any time, shuffling the order of the tiles.

PLAYING THE GAME

Only free tiles can be moved; your goal is to find matching pairs to be removed. A tile is considered "free" if it has no other tiles on top of it, and it can be removed by moving it to the right or left. This means that certain tiles may be exposed, but still landlocked between other tiles.

Only pairs of tiles can be removed; if you come across triplets of available matching tiles, you will have to select the best pair.

An exception to the matching rule, for Chinese-character faces—are members of the Flower and Season groups. Any flower or season can be matched with any other member of the family.

Move the cursor to the tile you want to remove and press the **A button** to make it start flashing; move the cursor to the matching pair and press the **A button** again to remove the pair.

If you make a mistake or change your mind, press the **B button** to cancel the previous move.

After you clear all of the tiles from the screen, a dragon will appear on the screen, bearing a message.

TYPES OF TILES

The 144 Shanghai tiles are made up of 108 Suit tiles, 12 Dragon tiles, 16 Wind, 4 Season and 4 Flower characters.

The Suit of Mahn. This is the suit of actors and people of letters, thought to stand for mankind.

The Suit of Dots. This suit is similar to the coins originally used by Chinese sailors when the game was first invented.

The Suit of Bamboo. This is the suit of victory and power.

The Suit of the Four Winds. There are characters for each of the directions of the wind: North. South, East and West.

The Suit of the Dragons. In the original game of Mah Jongg, there was the Dragon of the Sky, the Dragon of the Earth and the Dragon that hides within the hearts of Mankind.

The Suit of the Seasons. One character for each of the seasons, identified with the first three letters of each: SPR for Spring, SUM for Summer, AUT for Autumn and WIN for Winter. Any of the seasons tiles can be matched with any other season tile.

The Suit of Flowers. Thought to have been added by an ancient princess to bring romance to the game, they are Orchid, Plum, Mum and Bamboo. Any of the flower tiles can be matched with any other flower tile.

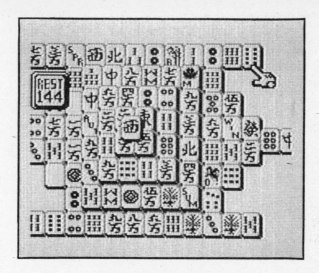

Classical Mah-Jongg.

HINTS

The game includes an expert who will help identify matching pairs. Press the **Select** button to enter the subscreen and then choose the second option for a hint. Press the **A button** to step through the possible pairs; press the **B button** to return to the game.

POWER PLAYER HINTS

No two layouts are the same. Study the layout before you begin.

In general, you should start by removing tiles from the deepest stacks in the middle.

MUSIC

To change the background music for the game, enter the subscreen and choose the BGM option; you will then be able to select from three tunes.

SECRET PASSWORDS

Here are three secret passwords.

One of them will not help you with the game at all: STF displays a list of credits for the people who designed the game.

Here's one that makes the game even more difficult to play: REV reverses the tiles so they cannot be seen until selected. Why would anyone want to choose this type of game? We can't imagine. It's impossible.

And finally, here's one that gives the easiest game in the deck, a set of Chinese characters that are relatively easy to match: MAN. And then if you want to make the game even easier, enter the code MAN and then choose the Face Option to display a set of numbers instead of characters—it's still a lot of fun.

Shanghai is a trademark of Activision, Inc. © 1986 Activision, Inc. Game pak © 1989 Hal Laboratory.

Tetris

AGE: 6 to Adult
DIFFICULTY: Apprentice-Master of the Game

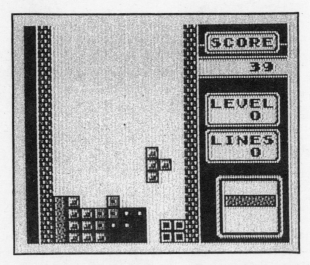

The T-Block will fill out the second line.

Tetris is the Rubik's Cube of computer software. It's not the most complex, the prettiest, or the most far-out game we've seen. But it is one of the most addictive challenges to come along, and it is perfectly suited to the small screen of the Game Boy. Just watch a player twisting and squeezing the handheld Nintendo sometime, just like it was a twistable cube. Try doing that with your 27-inch Sony sometime!

This game comes more or less straight from the Soviet Union, the first commercial software success from that country. And, conspiracy fans take note: Rubik's Cube also came from the communist world, from Czechoslovakia.

Actually, it's our theory that this game Tetris is the real reason behind the tremendous change going on in Russia and Eastern Europe these days. We see two possibilities: first that the Soviets have decided to give up on the idea of fighting with tanks and missiles and have instead decided to capture the hearts and minds of America and the rest of the world through this game; or second, that the leaders in the Kremlin are themselves so busy trying to score a Tetris that they haven't noticed their empire crumbling around them.

But seriously, Tetris is one impressive game. The Tetris game pak is included as a "free" game in the introductory Game Boy package. It is also available in a number of other formats, including a cartridge for the full-sized Nintendo Entertainment System as well as in versions for various computers including MS-DOS, Macintosh, Apple II, Atari ST, Commodore 64, and Amiga computers. You'll also find a version in the coin-operated arcades.

Tetris was designed by 30-year-old Alexi Paszitnov, a mathematics researcher in the Computer Center of the U.S.S.R. Academy of Scientists. The actual programming of the game was done on an IBM PC by 18-year-old whiz kid Vagim Gerasimov, a computer student at Moscow University.

The original Tetris was done in black and white and had no graphics or sound. Western programmers took over, adding quite a bit of commercial zip to the idea. They speeded up the game, added various difficulty levels and then set to work on the appearance of the game.

The version that made its way to the Game Boy is slightly less capable than the PC versions in its graphics, although the musical score (based on Russian folk songs) and sound effects (a satisfying clunk when a block fills out a line, plus assorted beeps and whistles for high scores) come across quite well using the Game Boy's digital stereo effects. Available only on the Game Boy is the special two-player version in which both contestants are connected to each other through the Video Link cable.

But, as we have said, this is a game that succeeds based on the fact that it is a great deal of fun—and a worthy challenge—to play. In fact, at the Software Publishers Association awards in 1989. the computer version of Tetris won no less than four Excellence in Software Awards: Best Entertainment Program, Best Action/Strategy Program, Best Original Game Achievement and Best Consumer Software. It beat out much more complex and detailed games including F-19 Stealth Fighter, Colony, Life and Death and Rocket Ranger.

The dangers of trying too hard for a Tetris.

About the Game

"It's really simple to play," say the instructions. And, so it is. But it is also very difficult to win.

You start with a blank playing field. From the top come tumbling one of seven different block shapes called Tetrads. There are four-block squares, four-block bars, Ls, Ts and Zs. As they descend, you can rotate them and move them left or right. The goal is to change and maneuver the blocks so that you end up with a completely filled straight row. After 10 rows disappear, you automatically move to the next level.

The Game Boy version of the Tetris includes three types of games: an Endurance competition; a high-score game, and a special two-player version where you connect your Game Boy to another machine and play head-to-head.

In an innovation for Nintendo games, you are also offered a choice of four audio options: three different songs or even no music at all except for the sound effects as pieces are fitted into place or thud into the wrong spot. The three musical selections each have a Russian theme. Choice A is something like a Russian classical piece; Choice B a brisk up-tempo Russian folk song (you can imagine Mario and Luigi performing a Kazatsky in gypsy clothes), and Choice C is a harpsichord-like melody.

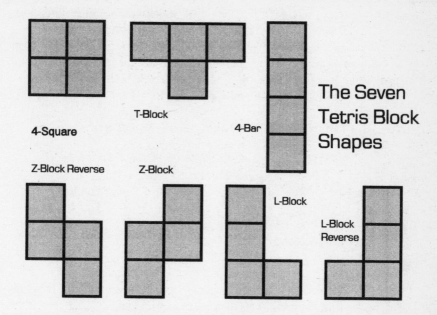

The game will record on the screen the names (as many as six letters) of the top three scorers for each Level. The high scores disappear when the power is turned off.

Nintendo of America and Tengen have been locked in a legal confrontation over the rights to market Tetris for the NES. As this book went to press, there was no court ruling as to which company could offer Tetris for the full-sized Nintendo Entertainment System. If you are an eagle-eyed shopper, you may find copies of Tengen's version of Tetris in some stores, despite the fact that a judge ordered the removal of those games until after he had ruled on the lawsuit between the two companies.

MANUFACTURER: Nintendo

NUMBER OF PLAYERS
1 (2nd player with Video Link to another Game Boy)

VIDEO LINK: Yes.

CHARACTERS:
You are the controller of the Tetris blocks. In the two-player version, one player becomes Mario and the other Luigi.

CONTROL PAD

Arrows: Left and Right move the falling block in those directions. The Down arrow can be used to speed up the fall of a block once you have it lined up. If your timing is good, you can also move a block left or right just after it has landed on the bottom row. Use this technique to sneak an L- or T-shaped block shape under an overhanging block.

"A" BUTTON: Rotates the falling block 90 degrees clockwise (to the right);

"B" BUTTON: Rotates the falling block 90 degrees counter-clockwise (to the left).

PAUSE

Press the **Start** button to pause the game; press it again to resume.

RESET

Press the **A, B, Select and Start buttons.**

STARTING THE GAME:

From the title screen, select a one-player or two-player game by moving the cursor using the Arrow keys and then pressing the Start button. The two-player version can only be selected when there are two Game Boys connected using the Video Link cable; both Game Boys must also have their own Tetris game pak in place.

ONE-PLAYER GAME

After you've selected the one-player game, you will next be offered a choice of **Game Type** and then **Music Type.** The standard settings of "A-Type" game and "A-Type Music" will flash; to accept them just press **Start.** To choose the "B-Type" game, use the Arrow keys to move the cursor. To move to the music selection, press the **A button** and then use the Arrow keys to select A, B, C or Off. Press **Start** to move to the Difficulty Selection Screen.

DIFFICULTY SELECTION

To start the game at the basic entry level, just press the **Start** button again.

In this screen, you can choose from among 10 levels, numbered from 0 to 9. The higher the level, the faster the blocks will fall.

In the B-Type game you can also choose how high a set of blocks you want to start with—the more blocks already on the screen, the more difficult an assignment you are setting for yourself. There are six levels here, numbered from 0 to 5.

A-TYPE GAME

The A-Type game is a test of endurance. Your goal is to accumulate as many points as possible by completing as many lines as you can. As you play, the level will gradually increase and the game will become harder.

The screen display for the A-Type game shows the following:

SCORE: Number of points you have earned by completing lines.
LEVEL: The speed for the block now falling.
LINES: The total number of lines completed in this game.
NEXT: An advance peek at the shape of the next block.

B-TYPE GAME

In this game, your goal is to complete 25 lines; the score is not calculated until you accomplish that task. You will be allowed to select the Level (falling speed for the blocks) and a HEIGHT (HIGH) setting (to control how many random blocks will already be in place at the bottom of the screen as the game begins. The level of the game will not change during a round.

The B-Type game is actually a pretty interesting way to work on your strategy. If you set the height setting to four or five, you've got a pretty fine mess to try to clear up. Your strategy here (see Ultimate Strategies for more details) is to clear from the top down to reduce the height of the pile.

The screen display for the B-Type game shows the following:

LEVEL: The speed for the block now falling.
HIGH: The height of the randomly placed blocks at the start of the game.
LINES: The number of lines remaining to be filled before you can win the game. (Counts down from 25.)
NEXT: An advance peek at the shape of the next block.

TWO-PLAYER GAME

The two-player version is unique to the Game Boy, adding a maddening new twist to the competition. In this game, the other player can send you some of his blocks.

You'll need two Game Boys for this competition, and they must be connected with the Video Link cable (one comes with each Game Boy set.) Be sure to plug in the cables with the power OFF to both machines and then turn them on.

The Game Boy player to first press **Start** will become Mario and the other player will be Luigi.

Just as in the one-player game, the object will be to complete lines. However, if you can score a double (completing two lines at once) you can send over one line of blocks to your opponent. If you score a triple, you can send two lines to your opponent. And, if you score a Tetris and complete four lines at once, you send all four lines over the cable to your opponent.

The two-player competition is won when either player completes 30 lines or when either player loses because his lines have been pushed all the way to the top of the screen. The first player to win four games is champion. If both players finish at the same time, it is declared a draw.

Another interesting feature of the two-player game is the ability to assign handicaps to better players, evening out the competition. Use a HIGH setting for the better player so that he or she will start out with a more difficult assignment.

SCORING POINTS

You will score the most points by competing two, three or four lines at once. And, the higher the block is dropped from, the more points you will score.

LEVEL	0	1	2	3	4	5	6	7	8	9
Single	40	80	120	160	200	240	280	320	360	400
Double	100	200	300	400	500	600	700	800	900	1000
Triple	300	600	900	1200	1500	1800	2100	2400	2700	3000
TETRIS	1200	2400	3600	4800	6000	7200	8400	9600	10800	12000

I ALWAYS WANTED TO KNOW

How in the world do I make a Tetris? There is only one way we can think of, and that is to complete four lines leaving only one open column that is continuous down through all four rows. Leave the opening clear, and hope for a straight line of four blocks to plug the gap all at once. But don't wait too long: you won't earn any points if the game is over.

SUPER SECRET!

There's a special super-round for those players who somehow are able to make it all the way through Level 9 and High setting 5 in Game B. We'd like to tell you what it is, but we haven't come close.

There is also a super-speed version of the game available right from the start. Just hold down one of the Arrow keys when you press the Start button to begin the game.

And, there are three special rewards for the super players. In the Type A game, when you score 100,000 points, a small rocketship will blast off

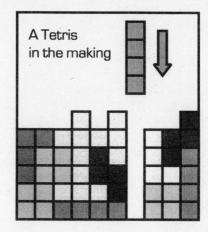

A Tetris
in the making

before your very eyes and tired fingers. Score 200,000 and there's an even larger ship.

In the Type B game, if you complete Level 9 at a Height setting of 9, first you'll see a grand Russian party with dancers and musicians, and then the Space Shuttle will be launched for your amusement. (It's an interesting mix, don't you think?) We have no idea what's hiding at higher levels—let us know if you reach them.

POWER PLAYER HINTS

Once you become comfortable with the basics of the game, try to sneak a peek at the shape of the upcoming block, displayed in the "NEXT" window. This should help you in your planning.

When you become a super Tetris player, you may want to make the game even more difficult (!) by removing the NEXT display. Do this by pressing the **Select** button during play. Press the **Select** button again to return display of the next game piece.

ULTIMATE STRATEGIES

The basic Tetris strategy, according to dedicated Tetris-Heads (Four-Heads?) is to build on the sides toward the center. This allows for more room for maneuvering when the piles get higher. The other way of looking at this advice is to put it this way: Don't put your pile of blocks in the center.

If you completely fill one line, you'll earn points and that line will disappear off the bottom of the screen making more room at the top. The

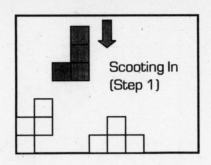

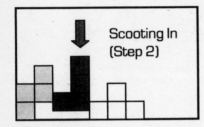

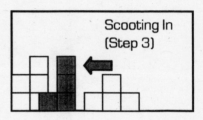

highest score for a particular move comes when you fill four lines at once—a Tetris. (The name of the game and the super move comes from the Greek word "tetra," meaning "four.") An example of a Tetris in the making can be seen in the accompanying picture. As you can see, the player here has left open a channel that can be neatly filled with a four-block bar. The danger of waiting for a bar in this manner is that the lines of blocks are beginning to get close to the top of the screen; when they reach the top row, the game is over.

However, don't think that the only way to fill a hole is with a four-square bar. If space begins to get tight at the top of the screen, you can still keep open the possibility of a Tetris by filling in the top row. There's a special maneuver we call "Opening the Door." The key here is the fact that rows, once filled, disappear and the rows above move down one row.

Another special move that you'll have to master is one we call "Scooting." There is a tiny amount of time between the moment a block hits bottom and the moment it is locked in place; in that time the block can be scooted left or right to plug an overhang. In the accompanying series illustrating scooting, we first see a descending Reverse L. Continue to move the block down, and at the moment it hits bottom, press the left arrow on the control pad to slide the L to the left.

There's also a super-secret scooting technique that defies the laws of physics: If you get the timing down exactly right and rotate a piece just above the point where it will settle, you can flip it through seemingly solid blocks. This allows for very precise fitting of a T, L or Z under a seemingly impossible overhang.

Here's a tip that will have more value in the highest rounds, where the speed of the tumbling blocks becomes faster and faster. When you rotate some Tetrads they will shift a row or more to the right. (Take a look at the position of a four-square bar in the vertical position and again after it has been turned.) At high speeds, therefore, you should build your blocks from the left side of the screen and leave room for tumblers to fall into the gaps on the right.

Wheel of Fortune

AGE: 8 years-Adult
DIFFICULTY: Apprentice

It's *Wheel of Fortune* on the Game Boy! It's a translation of the successful Nintendo game to the small screen! More than one thousand new word puzzles to solve! Stereo Sound! It's from Gametek! Can we stop shouting now?

Yes, here it is, straight off the television screen and right into the palms of your hands. This is not a particularly complex game—and neither is the television show upon which it is based—but for some reason, Wheel of Fortune has consistently drawn record-setting audiences. In fact, it is the highest-rated game show in the history of television.

We found the game to be more fun to play than to watch. According to the manufacturer, there are hundreds of different word puzzles to be solved in the game; the selections are chosen at random. Although there is always the possibility that you will end up with a puzzle you remember—there's even a very remote chance that you'll have the same puzzler more than once in the same game—we figure there's a fair amount of play time in Wheel of Fortune. Each time you reset the game, you reshuffle the deck.

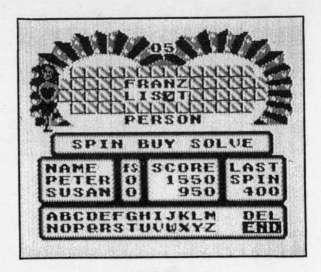

The game board.

We looked at a preproduction sample of the game and based our descriptions on the NES version of the game; some of the final details may have changed by the time the Game Boy cartridge arrives on the market.

MANUFACTURER: Gametek / (305) 935-3995

CONTROL PAD

Arrows: Move the on-screen cursor left or right to select letters for use in the game. Also used to make selections such as Yes/No or Spin/Vowel/Solve.

"A" or "B" BUTTONS: The action button. It is used to make selections from letters indicated by the on-screen cursor; it is also used to start the Wheel spinning.

NUMBER OF ROUNDS

Round 1 and 2: Basic "Wheel of Fortune" game play. Your winnings from the first round are transferred into the Total column of the second round, but are not considered current winnings.

Round 3: The Speed-up Round. Player 3 begins.

Round 4: Today's Big Prize. Only the player with the highest earnings gets to compete.

TIMING

Everything in this game is timed; if you choose to **Solve** a puzzle when there are a lot of letters to be filled in, you'll have to move very fast to get your solution into the computer before the clock runs down.

WHEELING FOR FORTUNE

At the start of the game, Player 1 can choose between a **Spin** of the Wheel, the purchase of a **Vowel** or the option to **Solve** the puzzle. You must make your choice quickly, before the timer in the lower left corner of the screen reaches 00.

If you choose **Spin,** the famous Wheel appears on the screen. You'll see (accompanied by a zippy sound effect) a moving horizontal "strength" bar at the top left of the screen. Pressing the **A or B buttons** while the bar is at the far right will give the Wheel a mighty spin; pushing the button when the bar is at the left gives it just a nudge.

Each of the wedges of the Wheel include a value, ranging from $150 to $1,000 in the first round, plus special wedges:

M00. The player will lose his or her next turn.

+00. The player gets a free spin, which can be used at once or used later on in that round.

B00. The player goes bankrupt, losing all winnings from the current round.

Next, the player is given the choice of entering a **Consonant, Buying a Vowel** or making an attempt to **Solve** the puzzle.

Vowels are the most prominent sound in a word, and consist of A, E, I, O and U (and sometimes Y) in English-language words.

A **Consonant**, broadly defined, is any letter that is not a vowel, the building blocks of words.

In the word "BOOK," for example, the B and K are consonants and the Os are the vowels, giving the word its character.

If you choose to enter a **Consonant,** you will be able to use the arrow keys to move the cursor on the screen left or right to select the letter you want to try on the board.

If you choose a letter that is included in the word or phrase that is in the puzzle, the girl in the cocktail dress will walk to the "wall" and turn the letters for you, ending with a polite little hand clap. You'll be given another spin of the wheel, too.

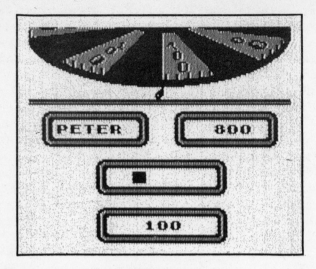

Going for a spin.

If you choose a letter that is not in the word, or if you choose a vowel instead of a consonant, or if you are so dense that you choose a letter someone else has already tried, your turn is ended.

If you want to enter a **Vowel** on the wall, you'll need to buy the right. Each vowel costs $250, and must come from winnings from the current round.

If you think you can **Solve the Puzzle,** choose that option. When you select Solve with the arrow keys and press the **A or B buttons,** you'll see another version of the puzzle at the bottom of the screen. Use the cursor keys to select the missing letters, working from left to right and pressing the **A or B button** when the letter you want is highlighted. When you think you have the puzzle completely filled in, move the cursor to End and press the **A or B buttons** again.

You've got to work quickly in this part of the game, since you are playing against the timer. Spelling counts, too. If you misspell any part of the word or phrase, your guess is judged to be incorrect and the turn passes to the next player. But if you get it right, the girl on the screen will clap!

THE SPEED-UP ROUND

In Round 3, the Wheel will spin all by itself at the start; the value of the segment in which it stops indicates the amount of money each consonant will be worth in that round. Each player will take turns guessing consonants and will earn the indicated amount of money for each correct guess. Correct vowels do not earn any bonus money.

After each correct guess in this round, the player will be offered a chance to solve the puzzle.

At the end of the round, the player with the highest total earnings—including Rounds 1, 2 and 3, gets to play in Round 4, the big enchilada.

ROUND 4

First, you'll get to choose the big prize. Selections include trips to Disney World, sports cars, boats and other game show-type prizes. (Before you get too excited: this is all just a game; Vanna Whatshername will not show up at your front door with the keys to a Porsche if you win.)

In the game itself, the player is shown the category for the puzzle, and then allowed to choose five consonants and one vowel. Move quickly, since the timer is running.

Our friend will sashay up to the wall and turn over the letters in the puzzle that match your guesses, and then you will be given as many chances as are possible within the timed countdown to solve.

·4·
Gym Bag

Baseball
AGE: 6 to Adult
DIFFICULTY: Apprentice-Hot Dog

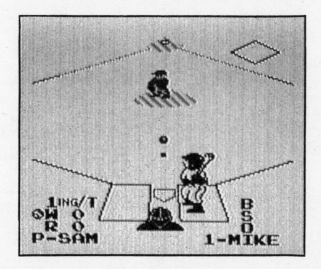

Here comes the pitch.

Welcome to the littlest of leagues. Baseball is a very complex game, but that hasn't stopped dozens of developers from trying to come up with electronic versions.

Fielding is "auto defense" for most routine balls, meaning the computer will help out from time to time, but the head-to-head competition against the programmed opponent makes for a tough game.

And, the "point of view" differences between what two human players will see on a pair of Game Boys is something that cannot be duplicated on the big NES system.

There is a lot of programming beneath the surface in this game, available from Nintendo, although we found a lot more substance and game value in Jaleco's Bases Loaded GB.

MANUFACTURER: Nintendo

NUMBER OF PLAYERS

1 or 2 players. 2-player game can only be selected if two Game Boys are used, each with its own Baseball game pak, connected by the Video Link cable. In the 1-player game, you compete against the computer. In the 2-player version, each contestant controls his own team.

CHARACTERS

The home team White Bears and the visiting Red Eagles baseball teams, available in slightly different American and Japanese versions. The star pitcher on the Bears is some guy named Mario; the Eagles rely heavily on a right-handed fastballer named Luigi.

STARTING THE GAME

At the start of the game, you can choose between USA and JPN (Japanese) modes, and can choose to leave background music (BGM) on or turn it off. Use the arrow keys to move the cursor to your selection and then press the **Start** or the **A buttons.**

Next you will be able to choose which of the two available teams you would like to manage. The White Bears are always the visiting team, and bat first; the Red Eagles are in the field.

The final selection is the choice of a starting pitcher. Use the arrow keys to move the cursor to the pitcher you want to use, and then press the **A button** or **Start** to begin the game.

PAUSE

Press the **Start** button to call a time-out. Press the button two times more to resume play. The **Start** button is also used to call in a relief pitcher.

BASE SELECTION

To move the runner or throw the ball to a particular base, use the arrow keys in combination with the specified **A or B buttons** as follows:

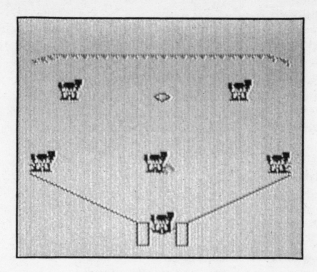

The fielders salute the crowd.

Right arrow. First base   **Up arrow.** Second base
Left arrow. Third base   **Down arrow.** Home plate

PITCHING

Arrows: *Before releasing the ball:* moves the pitcher left or right on the pitching mound.

Once the ball is released: the left and right arrows can be used to affect the flight of the ball to the inside or outside of the plate. The up and down arrows can be used to affect the speed of the ball; the up arrow slows the pitch, the down arrow speeds it up.

"A" BUTTON: Press once to set the pitcher in position on the pitching mound. Press a second time to throw the ball.

"B" BUTTON: Changes display to field screen. Used in pick-off attempts.

Relief pitchers: To change pitchers in the middle of a game, press the **Start** button twice. The name of available relief pitchers will be shown. Use the arrow keys or the **Select** button to choose a new pitcher, and then press the **A button** to make the pitching change.

Pick-off move: To attempt to pick a runner off his base, press the **B button** to change to the field display. Then press the **A button** and the control arrow for the base you want to throw to.

BATTING

Arrows: Move the batter left or right within the batting box.

"A" BUTTON: Pressed firmly, makes the batter swing. Tapped quickly, the batter will attempt a bunt.

Pinch hitting: To change batters, press the **Start** button to call time, and then press the button again to display a list of available pinch hitters. Use the arrow keys or the **Select** button to choose a new hitter. Press the **A button** to put the new batter in the game.

RUNNING

To advance to a new base, press the arrow pad for the base you want to and press the **B button.**

To return to the previous base to avoid being tagged out, press the arrow key for the base you want and press the **A button.** Once the runner comes close to a base, he will automatically try to slide; once he is in a slide, he cannot be recalled to the previous base.

To attempt to steal a base, press the **B button** and the appropriate arrow key while the pitcher has begun his windup.

FIELDING

The game is set up so that fielders will automatically catch most "routine" fly balls and popups. You can just watch as the fielder moves into position and raises his hand to indicate he has the ball in sight.

Balls hit on the ground, fly balls down the left and right foul lines and long fly balls that strike the fence usually require the player to chase them with the fielder. Use the arrow keys to move the fielder into position; when he comes to the ball, it automatically goes into his throwing hand.

When an infielder gets the ball, he can throw it to any base by pressing the appropriate arrow key and the **A button.** The infielder can also run to a base with the ball; just press the appropriate arrow key and the **B button.** While running, you can decide to throw the ball; press an arrow key and the **A button.**

Outfielders can throw the ball to a selected base using a arrow key and the **A button,** but cannot run to a base with the ball.

USA vs. JPN TEAMS:

The American and Japanese batting orders are subtly different. Pitchers on the American teams are stronger and faster, relying more on their fastballs than on curveballs.

There are more left-handed players in USA mode; the Red Eagles on the American side having 7 southpaws and just 4 righties. A good strategy, if you are the manager of the White Bears, would be to use a left-handed pitcher against the Eagles and pitch inside.

We ran a computer analysis of the statistics on the two teams, in their USA and JPN versions. Both of the White teams (USA and JPN Bears) have Composite Batting Averages of .293; both Red teams (USA and JPN Eagles) bat .291 as a team. All four teams share the same Composite Batting Ability at 2.91 and Composite Batting Skill at 2.18.

The only slight differences come among the pitchers.

	Composite Pitching Stamina	Composite Pitching Speed	Composite Pitching Changeup
USA WHITE BEARS	1.5 (B++)	1.75 (B+)	2.5 (C++)
JPN WHITE BEARS	1.75 (B+)	2.75 (C+)	1.5 (B++)
USA RED EAGLES	1.5 (B++)	1.75 (B+)	2.5 (C++)
JPN RED EAGLES	2.0 (B)	2.75 (C+)	1.5 (B++)

In pitching stamina, an A indicates the strongest pitcher, one most likely to be able to fire those fastballs for a complete game. Pitching speed uses A to indicate the hardest fastball. Pitching changeup uses A as the mark of the pitcher with the best curveball and screwball.

Game play in both modes is the same. You'll notice that the Japanese scoreboard lists strikes first, then balls; a "full count" in Japan is 2-and-3. Also, the radar gun on the Japanese pitchers will display speed in kilometers per hour.

2-PLAYER GAME
An exciting variation of the Baseball game pak comes when you hook up two Game Boys for head-to-head competition over the Video Link cable. In addition to a second game Boy, you'll need two Baseball game paks and the cable. As with all Video Link games, connect the cable and install the game paks with the power OFF and then turn both machines on.

GROUND RULES
Just like the major leagues, Game Boy Baseball has its own special ground rules for the stadium. They include:

1. If one team goes ahead by 10 or more runs, the game is declared over.
2. If the game is tied at the end of 9 innings, a 10th inning will be played. If neither team is ahead after 10 innings, the game is declared a draw.

SUPER SECRET!

The pitcher and catcher in this game are really not all that good at holding runners on base or throwing them out in a steal attempt. So, include the stolen base as an important element of your offensive repertoire.

POWER PLAYER HINTS

Most of the same theories that apply to major league baseball can be used in this game.

Note that the batting order does not assign fielding positions. Therefore, if you wanted to immediately pinch hit for the weakest player on your team you can do so without having to worry about replacing him in the field.

Most managers prefer to be the home team, not just because the crowd is behind you. Having the sudden-death bottom-of-the-ninth inning for tie games can be a considerable advantage. The Red Eagles are the home team in both the USA and JPN modes.

Baseball game pak © 1989 Nintendo of America Inc.

Bases Loaded Game Boy

AGE: 6 years to Adult
DIFFICULTY: Apprentice-Hot Dog

These are the big leagues on the little Game Boy. The original Bases Loaded game pak for the Nintendo Entertainment System brought the majors to the video game screen; that success was followed by a most worthy sequel called Bases Loaded II: Second Season.

The Game Boy version is a tour de force of mini-programming. We looked at a very early preproduction copy of the program, but we still had a ball.

MANUFACTURER: Jaleco / (708) 480-1811

NUMBER OF PLAYERS

1, or 2 players in head-to-head play with Video Link cable.

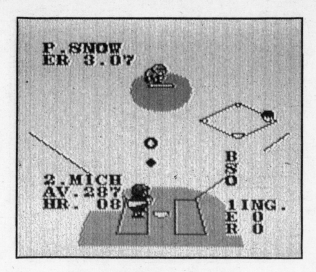

The view from the batter's box.

GAME PLAY

The actions of the control pad depend on the playing mode: in the field, on the pitching mound, on the basepaths or at bat.

PITCHING

Throwing a pitch is a two-step process.

First, use the left or right arrow key to select the location for the pitch. Against a right-handed batter, the right arrow will bring the pitch inside and the left arrow will move the pitch to the outside; for a left-handed batter the inside/outside arrows act in the opposite manner. Press the **A button** once the pitch selection has been made.

Next, select the type of pitch. Press the arrow key for the pitch you have chosen together with the **A button** to put the pitcher into his motion. The pitch selections, shown in the accompanying picture, are as follows:

Up. Fastball.
Down. Change-up. (Looks more like an underhand pitch to us.)
Left. Curve.
Right. Screwball.
Up/Right. Fast Screwball.
Up/Left. Fast Curve.
Down/Right. Slow Screwball.
Down/Left. Slow Curve.

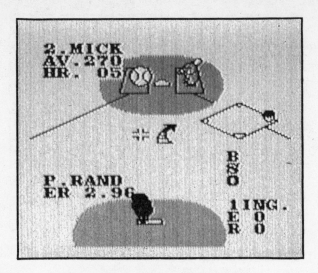

The view from the pitcher's mound.

There is also at least one mystery pitch for each hurler. One of the throws we played against uncorked a corkscrew of a pitch that almost mesmerized us; it looked worse than it was, though, since we were able to hit it anyway once we figured out the timing.

FIELDING AND THROWING

Arrows: Move the nearest fielder toward the ball using the control arrows.

"A" BUTTON: To throw the ball, press the **A button** and the arrow key that points to the appropriate base.

The bases are assigned as follows:

Right. First Base.

Up. Second Base.

Left. Third Base.

Down. Home Plate.

If the arrow key is not pressed, the ball will automatically be thrown to first base.

"B" BUTTON: For a Jumping Catch, press the **B button** while the ball is overhead.

For a Diving Catch, press the **B button** and the arrow key in the direction you want your fielder to dive.

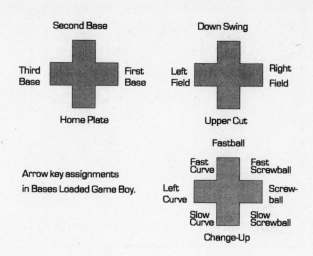

Second Base

Third
Base

First
Base

Home Plate

Down Swing

Left
Field

Right
Field

Upper Cut

Fastball

Arrow key assignments
in Bases Loaded Game Boy.

Fast
Curve

Fast
Screwball

Left
Curve

Screw-
ball

Slow
Curve

Slow
Screwball

Change-Up

HITTING

For a basic swing, press the **A button.**

To attempt a bunt, tap the **A button** before the pitch is thrown. To attempt to direct the ball, tap the **A button** again as the ball passes over the plate.

Choosing the type of swing requires a bit of extra coordination. Before the pitcher goes into his windup, press the **Select** button. You will see crosshairs just above home plate. Press and hold the arrow key on the control pad to select your swing, and then press the **A button** to swing when the ball is over the plate. The special swings are:

Up. A down swing to attempt to hit the ball on the ground.
Down. An upper cut, to attempt to hit the ball in the air.
Left. A swing aiming for the left side of the infield.
Right. A swing aiming for the right side of the infield.

STEALING

To send a baserunner in an attempt to steal a base, when the pitcher releases the ball press the arrow key toward the base you want to steal and press the **B button** repeatedly.

To return to a base, press the **A button** and the arrow pad in the direction representing the base you want to go to.

To attempt a hit-and-run, work both the **A and B buttons** at the same time.

A deep fly to left field.

PICKOFF PLAY

To attempt to pick a runner off the base, press the **B button** before the type of pitch has been selected. Throw the ball to first base by pressing the **A button.** To throw to a different base, press the **A button** together with the appropriate arrow key.

SUBSTITUTIONS

To bring in a relief pitcher, call Time Out by pressing the Start button. Press the **A button** to display the player selection screen; use the up or down arrow keys to select the player you wish to use and press the A **button** to make your choice.

To bring in a pinch hitter, call Time Out by pressing the Start button. Press the **A button** to display the player selection screen; use the up or down arrow keys to select the player you wish to use and press the A **button** to make your choice.

PAUSE

Press the Start button to call Time Out. Pitching and pinch hitter changes can be made during this time. Press the Start button again to resume play.

POWER PLAYER HINTS

A bunt is a pretty good offensive weapon. Use it to build a run by moving a runner into scoring position with 0 or 1 out. If you can master the technique of tapping the **A button** to move the bat at the moment of contact, you may be able to beat out bunts for singles with fair regularity.

In the early version of the game that we worked with, we found three different lineups of players. We expect that there will be some changes in the names of the players—especially among the players on the West Team. You may see players with the same stats but different names in the final version. Here is what we found:

TEAM ONE

Starters

COOK	.296	HR	31
MICH	.287	HR	8
BARK	.334	HR	49
CLAR	.296	HR	42
PLAN	.296	HR	12
ILLS	.261	HR	7
STIF	.252	HR	5
WOLF	.387	HR	1
POE	.296	HR	12

Pinch Hitters

CLAN	.234	HR	13
KING	.261	HR	10
HAHN	.252	HR	7
BLUE	.270	HR	9

Pitchers

RAND	2.96	ERA
COLL	3.07	ERA
THER	2.61	ERA
SHAK	3.87	ERA

TEAM TWO

Starters

MOUS	.287	HR	12
MICK	.270	HR	5
HUEY	.307	HR	27
DEWE	.296	HR	29
LOUE	.287	HR	21
PLIK	.287	HR	10
FRAK	.237	HR	7
MAZE	.252	HR	8
CLAR	.234	HR	5

Pitchers

SHOW	4.07	ERA
CARY	3.16	ERA
MYER	2.70	ERA
ROBB	3.07	ERA

TEAM THREE

Starters

SETZ	.296	HR 15
RYBY	.361	HR 2
CONE	.307	HR 38
MADD	.316	HR 43
BLUE	.307	HR 37
LUTZ	.261	HR 8
BERK	.252	HR 5
MAIN	.270	HR 7
ZUGG	.307	HR 10

Pinch Hitters

PROP	.296	HR 9
NABY	.252	HR 10
KAZ	.261	HR 8
SKAJ	.243	HR 11

Bases Loaded Game Boy is a trademark of Jaleco Ltd. © 1990 Jaleco Ltd. Game Boy is a trademark of Nintendo of America Inc.

Golf

AGE: 8 years-Adult
DIFFICULTY:Novice-Apprentice

At last! They've found a way to play two full rounds of 18 holes of championship golf, complete with manicured fairways, tangled roughs and mucky ponds and a full bag of clubs—but you won't have to leave the clubhouse. In fact, you could play this course on a jet plane or in the backseat of a car.

The cleverly named Golf game, from Nintendo, is a nicely done version of electronic golf for play on the Game Boy machine.

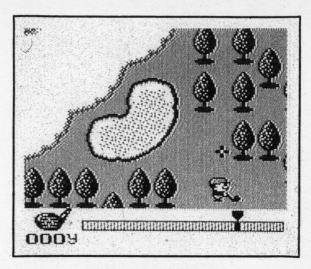

Approaching the green.

MANUFACTURER: Nintendo

NUMBER OF PLAYERS

1. Two-player game requires two copies of the game pak, two Game Boy machines and the Video Link cable.

CHARACTERS

The little guy in the golfer's hat looks remarkably like one of those zany Italian plumbers . . . we think his name is Mario. Must be his day off from rescuing princesses. Actually, each player can enter his or her name onto the scorecard, and the name, current game results and best score will be maintained by the game pak even when the power is turned off. You can enter the names of two players, but with a single copy of the game pak you will have to choose one or the other player for a particular game. In any case, the picture remains the same . . . this odd-looking little Italian plumber.

STARTING THE GAME

Your options at game start are:

Continue. To resume a previously suspended round of golf by one of the two players stored in the game pak's memory.

New Game. To begin a new game from the first hole, using a new player name.

Best Score. Selecting this option shows the scorecard for the best game played by the selected, registered player for either or both of the courses in the game. If you delete the player name by entering a new identity, the best scores are also deleted.

RESET

To reset the game and return to the title screen at any point, press the **A and B buttons** along with the **Select** and **Start** buttons.

CONTROL PAD

Arrows: Move the cursor, for different purposes at different stages of the game:

PLAY SCREEN
Up and Down selects clubs.
Left or Right sets the shot direction.

HOLE SCREEN
PUTTING GREEN SCREEN
Scrolls the screen up, down, left or right.

"A" BUTTON: The first press of the **A button** determines the stroke power. The second press brings the club down to hit the ball.

"B" BUTTON: Switches between the Play, Hole and Green screen during play.

START BUTTON: Enters selections when you are choosing from menus.
Displays the current score during play.

SELECT: Allows you to go to the Save screen during play to store the current game.

NUMBER OF COURSES

There are two 18-hole courses in the game pak, one set in Japan and the other in the United States. Both courses are 72-par; the U.S. course is longer, at 6,749 yards total while the Japanese course is 6,453 yards for 9 holes out and 9 holes in.

The longest hole on the U.S. course is the 6th, a par-5 556-yard challenge. Shortest American hole is lucky 13, at 147 yards for a par of 3. On the Japanese course, the long honors go to the 13th at 545 yards with a par of 5; the shortest Japanese hole is 11, at 142 yards and a par of 3.

PLAY SCREEN

The Play Screen is the view from the current location of the ball. This is where you will actually select your club and take a swing. If you press

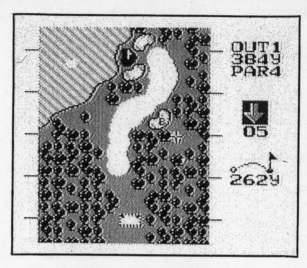

A bird's eye view of the course.

the **A button,** the player will appear next to the ball and the shot indicator will be displayed at the bottom of the screen; if you press the **B button** the display will change to the Hole Screen.

At middle left of the screen you will see the number of strokes you have taken in the current hole. Below that is an indication of the number of strokes over or under par you are for the game thus far.

At the bottom left of the screen is the value of par for the game to this point. To the right of that number is the distance, in yards, from the present location of the ball to the cup.

At bottom center is an indication of the current direction of the wind and its strength.

At the bottom right is the name of the currently selected club.

HITTING THE BALL

Ordinary Swings. This is, after all, the whole purpose we are gathered here, right? Your first assignment is to determine the direction in which the ball will begin its flight. Do this using the Left or Right arrow keys.

Next you must select the appropriate golf club using the Up or Down arrow keys. See: "I Always Wanted to Know."

Now, press the **A button** to get ready to strike the ball. At the bottom of the screen you will see the Shot Indicator. Press the **A button** again to draw back the club; press the **A button** to start the swing forward and press the **A button** a third time to hit the ball. The further back you pull the club the stronger your swing will be. The closer to the position of the ball the club is when you hit the button for the third time the truer the shot will be.

Which brings us to the topic of **Hooks** and **Slices.** A slice is a shot that curves to the right; a hook curves to the left. If you hit the **A button** for the third time when the club is to the left of the dark area in the Shot Indicator, the ball will slice. If you hit the ball when the indicator is to the right of the dark area, the ball will hook.

To hit the ball higher than ordinary (to loft it over a tree or other obstacles) hold the Down arrow during the swing.

To hit the ball lower than ordinary (to go under an overhanging tree or other obstacle) press the Up arrow during the swing.

Putting a **Back Spin** on a ball keeps it from rolling very far after it lands. This is not all that easy: first of all, you must hit the ball straight on without any hook or spin. That done, you must be pressing the Left or Right arrow at the moment you hit the ball. If you have done this correctly, the words "Back Spin" will be displayed at the bottom of the screen.

HOLE SCREEN

The Hole Screen is an overhead view of as much of the entire hole as can be presented; you may need to use the arrow keys to move around the display "window" that looks down on the hole. If you press the **A button,** the display will return to the Play Screen; if you press the **B button** again, you will move on to the Green Screen.

You will see along the right side of the screen the same information as is displayed in the Play screen.

GREEN SCREEN

This is a closeup view of the green. You'll be able to more precisely note the location of the pin and hole and see ground slopes and other special features of the green.

Press either the **A or B button** to return to the Play Screen.

Putting follows slightly different rules: Press the **A button** to move the club back and then press the **A button** a second time to swing and hit the ball. The farther to the left you bring the club, the stronger your swing will be.

You will find three different kinds of "landscaping" on the greens. Areas that are blank are flat and the ball will roll straight. Areas with small V-shaped arrows have a slight slope, in the direction of the head of the V. Areas with larger arrows are more steeply sloped.

TRAINING MODE

To enter the course and practice on any hole, choose the training mode. From the Title Screen, press the Down arrow and Start. Use the Up or Down arrow keys to pick the course and the Left or Right arrow keys to choose the hole you want to work on. Use the Reset (**A+B+Start+Select**) to return to the title screen.

I ALWAYS WANTED TO KNOW

How in the world do I get my friend's name and his embarrassing scores out of the cartridge? Hmmm . . . does he embarrass you because he's so bad or because he's so good? Whatever. To change one of the registered players, go to the Game Select screen and select New Game, select the name you want to replace and press the **A button.** The last step is to enter a new name. Then get yourself a new partner, okay?

Which club, when? The right one, now, of course. In general, you want a wood for a tee shot, a wood or an iron for a shot from the fairway, an iron or a wedge from the rough or a bunker and a putter for the green. There are 14 clubs in your bag (still, the Game Boy seems so light). Although the actual distance they will drive a ball will be determined by such factors as the strength of your swing, the accuracy of impact of the club and ball and the wind direction; here are the average distances for each type:

1W (Wood)	240 yards	6I	150 yards
3W	225 yards	7I	135 yards
4W	215 yards	8I	120 yards
1I (Iron)	205 yards	9I	110 yards
3I	190 yards	PW (Pitching Wedge)	
4I	180 yards		90 yards
5I	165 yards	SW (Sand Wedge)	
			70 yards
		PT (Putter)	
			30 yards

THE 2-PLAYER GAME

If you use the Video Link cable to connect two Game Boys, each with its own copy of the Golf game pak, you can enter into Match Play. In match Play, a winner is declared for each hole. If you sink the ball in the cup in fewer strokes than your opponent, you are Up a hole; if you and your opponent are tied for number of holes won, you are Even, and if you have won fewer games than your opponent, you are Down holes.

The 2-player game also includes the ability to assign Handicaps, from 0 to 18. Each hole has an assigned handicap; if you pick a handicap of 6, for example, you will be given a one-stroke advantage over your opponent on all holes with a handicap of 6 or less.

If you have fallen so far behind on a particular hole that you stand no chance of winning, you can press the Select button to display the Give Up option to advance to the next hole.

If the two players are tied at the end of a round, you will go into a Sudden Death competition where play will continue until one wins a hole.

SCORING

Each time you swing at the ball you will record one stroke, and in stroke play the contestant who completes the course in the fewest number of strokes wins.

If you shoot a ball out bounds (off the course) the ball will be returned to your original position for another shot, but you will be penalized one stroke.

If you land your ball in the water, you will be penalized one shot and will shoot again from the edge of the water.

The counter for each hole will stop at 50! If you're still trying to sink the ball after that many tries, keep on going, secure in the knowledge that 50 will be the worst score you will record.

POWER PLAYER HINTS

Pay attention to the wind direction on drives. If there is a strong wind across the course, you may want to intentionally hook or slice the ball.

Look at the landscaping on the greens and try not to let the slopes send your ball in the wrong direction.

CONTINUING

The Save and Continue functions of Golf work only for the 1-player game. While you are playing, the computer is automatically keeping a record of all of your play; if you were to merely turn off the power to the game, your statistics would have been recorded to memory.

To continue a saved game, go to the Game Select screen and move the cursor in front of the name of the player you want to be. Then press the Start button.

Malibu Beach Volleyball

AGE: 7 years-Adult
DIFFICULTY:Novice-Apprentice

Volleyball, by the beautiful sea.

Every place has to have some claim to fame, and Malibu Beach in California is proud of its sand-court volleyball. On the one hand, this is fun-in-the-sun play on the beach; on the other hand, this is in-your-face spikes and up-your-nose dives.

You will be able to select your preferred league, match and music from the opening screen. We appreciated the assistance of the referee, and especially her bikini—err, her official beach umpire uniform.

MANUFACTURER: Activision / (415) 329-7699

NUMBER OF PLAYERS

1 or 2. The two-player game requires two copies of the Malibu Beach Volleyball game cartridge, a pair of Game Boys and the Video Link cable.

CHARACTERS

You can be American, Brazilian, Italian or Japanese for the day. In fact, you can be the entire team.

CONTROL PAD:

SERVING THE BALL

You will have to learn how to time your toss, jump and hit to properly serve the ball. If you miss the ball, the referee will declare a "Side Out" and the other time will receive the ball for service. You will also lose your serve if you place the ball outside of your opponent's court before it bounces, if you serve the ball into the net or touch the net with the serve.

Arrows: Move the server Left or Right along the base line before the serve.

"A" BUTTON: For a regular serve, press the **A button** once to toss the ball and a second time to hit the ball. To aim the serve, press the Left or Right arrows as you press the **A button.**

"B" BUTTON: For a power serve, press the **B button** to toss the ball high, press the **B button** a second time to make the server jump, and then press the **A button** to hit the ball. To aim a power serve, hold down the Left or Right arrow when you make the server jump and hit the ball.

RETURNING THE BALL

The object of the game, of course, is to get the ball safely back over the net. However, you're not likely to win the game if you merely pop the ball over the net neatly into the hands of your opponents. A much better strategy involves a smash, or a one-two setup to a spike. Your players can pass the ball back and forth two times before sending it over the net (a total of three touches of the ball).

In the P1 VS COM and P1 VS P2 games you control two players at a time. When the ball first comes over the net, you will automatically be placed in control of the player nearest the ball. If you pass the ball to your other player, the control will automatically pass to him or her.

In the P1 and P2 VS COM game, you will control one of the players and the other human player will control the other. You will control the same player throughout the game.

When the ball is in the air, you will see an "X" where it is likely to land. You'll also see the shadow of the ball as it moves across the court.

Arrows: Positions your player under the ball using the Left, Right, Up or Down arrows.

"A" BUTTON: Press the **A button** to hit the ball. To hit the ball directly over the net without a setup, press the Up arrow with the **A button.**

"B" BUTTON: Makes your player jump. To spike the ball, press the **B button** to jump and then press the **A button** at the top of the jump to slam the ball down on the other side of the net.

DEFENSE

To attempt to block an opponent's spike, bring your player directly in front of the spiker and press the **B button** to jump as he sends the ball over the net.

PAUSE

To pause the game, press the Start button. Press the button again to resume play.

RESET

To reset the game press the **A and B buttons**, together with the Start and Reset buttons.

SCORING

In a one-game match, the team to first score 15 points wins the game. You must win by two points or more, up to a score of 17. You will change sides when the total score is a multiple of 8.

In a three-game match, you will play a best-of-three match to 12 points, changing sides after each of the first two games. If there is a third game, you will change sides when the score is a multiple of 5. You must win by two points, up to a score of 14.

You will only be able to score points when it is your serve. If you are serving and lose the volley, the serve will go to the other side without a point being awarded.

NUMBER OF TEAMS

There are four teams in the cartridge, with the American team being the true powerhouse and the Italians the roundheels. The Brazilian and Japanese teams are evenly matched. Here are the team characteristics:

	USA	BRA	JPN	ITA
Spiking Strength	4	2	3	1
Running Speed	4	3	2	1

POWER PLAYER HINTS

In a two-player game, the contestant who first presses the Start or **A button** will be P1. It's not really such a big deal who goes first—take turns if you are really competitive about it. Try to avoid a situation where both players press Start or the **A button** at the same moment, since this may royally confuse the Game Boy.

There is no Practice Mode per se, although you can set yourself up with the easiest competition by choosing the Women's League and playing Italy, which is a bit of a pushover. To keep playing Italy, reset the game after the match.

Use the arrow keys to make your selections from the league, team and music selections and then press the **A button** to lock in your choice. If you press the **A button** before you have made a selection, the Game Boy computer will make all of your decisions for you.

Malibu Beach Volleyball is a trademark of Activision. © 1990 Activision. Game contents © 1989 Tokyo Shoseki Ltd.

NBA All-Star Challenge

AGE: 7 years-Adult
DIFFICULTY: Apprentice-Hot Dog

There's a good name attached to this one: NBA, as in National Basketball Association; All-Star, as in Michael Jordan, Larry Bird, Charles Barkley, Isiah Thomas, Patrick Ewing, James Worthy and lots of other super pros, and Challenge, as in a sweaty palms set of head-to-head competitions as well as other hoop contests.

You can play against the computer, or against another player with his own copy of the NBA All-Star Challenge cartridge and a second Game Boy, connected with the Video Link cable.

Competitions include half-court 1-on-1 games and tournaments; your choice of player will affect their shooting and defensive abilities. The player selection screen includes digitized photos of the stars and some of their vital

One-on-one.

NBA foul shooting.

game statistics. Also included are Around-the-World shooting contests (some call this game "Horse") and a Foul-Shooting Contest.

We looked at an early preproduction copy of the game.

NFL

AGE: 8 years-Adult
DIFFICULTY: Apprentice

Football has been defined as war with rules. The real NFL rule book and the player and coaches' play book are about the size of a big-city telephone book. The Game Boy version of NFL football presents a much simplified but still enjoyable version of professional football.

You'll get to select offenses and defenses and control the action of your tiny electronic players right in the palm of your hand. Add the Video Link for a head-to-head confrontation with a friend.

We especially like the tiny little ref who comes trotting down the field at the end of each play and blows his even tinier little whistle.

We suspect that this game will appeal mostly to the serious football fan, interested in testing out various offensive and defensive patterns in particular situations. The more casual fan may find there is not enough action in this program, despite its huge underlying database of football strategies.

The Story of Football

The rules of football have evolved over more than a century in the United States from its distant roots in the game of rugby.

The football field is 100 yards long with 10-yard end zones at each end of the field. The field is 53 1/3 yd (160 feet) wide. A team is made up of 11 players on each side. Teams advance the ball by running with it, passing (throwing) it or kicking it. The lines at each end of the field are called goal lines, and the object of the game is for a player to cross the other team's goal line with the ball and score a touchdown. A touchdown is worth 6 points, while a ball kicked through the uprights of the goalposts in the endzone is worth 3 points. A second kind of kicking point is a Point After Touchdown, worth 1 point.

Football made its first appearance as a college game. Collegians originally played rugby, but the sport was considered so grueling that it was barred from Harvard University in 1860. In 1869, two New Jersey univer-

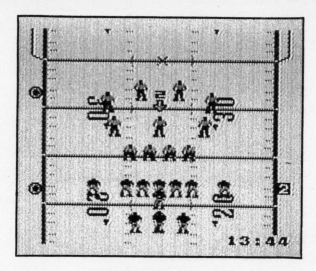

The electronic gridiron.

sities, Rutgers and Princeton, played what is considered the first intercollegiate game in the United States, although the game they played differed greatly from present-day football. There were 25 players on each side, and the scoring was decided by goals, not touchdowns, conversions, and field goals. (Rutgers won, by the way, although Princeton won a rematch a week later.)

The first recorded professional football game was in 1895, when a team from Latrobe, Pennsylvania, played against a team from nearby Jeannette. In 1919 the foundation of what would become the National Football League was made in Canton, Ohio. A second professional league, the All-America Football Conference, was founded in 1946. That league was absorbed by the NFL in 1950.

Football began to soar in popularity in the 1950s with the arrival of television. In 1960 the American Football League was formed, in direct competition with the NFL for players, fans and TV money. The two leagues signed a merger agreement in 1966 (they became one league in 1970) and the first Super Bowl was played in January of 1967.

Despite its tremendous popularity in the United States, until recently the game had not had much success off the North American continent. (Canadians play a slightly different version of the sport.) But in recent years, American football teams have toured in Europe and Asia, and new professional leagues are developing there.

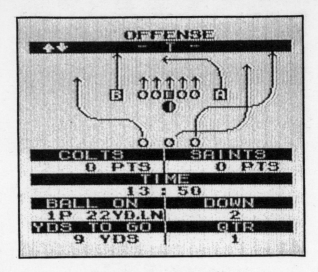

The offensive play screen.

MANUFACTURER: Konami / (708) 215-5111

NUMBER OF PLAYERS
1 player against the computer, or 2 players in head-to-head competition using the Video Link cable. In a 1-player game, you will receive the ball and begin the game on offense; in a 2-player game, whichever player acts quicker to select his or her team will start the game on offense.

PAUSE
Press the Start button to call time out; press the button again to resume play.

NUMBER OF TEAMS
The names of all 28 teams of the National Football League are available; game play for each of the teams is the same. The teams are:

49ers	Chiefs	Oilers
Bears	Colts	Packers
Bengals	Cowboys	Patriots
Bills	Dolphins	Raiders
Broncos	Eagles	Rams
Browns	Falcons	Redskins
Buccaneers	Giants	Saints

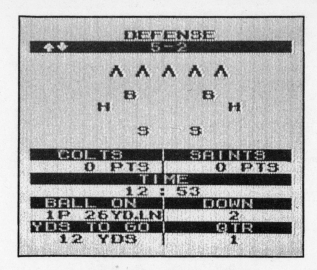

The defensive play screen.

Cardinals	Jets	Seahawks
Chargers	Lions	Steelers
		Vikings

In the one-player game, you first select the team that you wish to control and then select a team for the Game Boy to manage. Your opponent, by the way, is referred to as the "CPU", which is a computer term that stands for "Central Processing Unit."

TIMING

There are two time clocks available: Normal gives four 15-minute quarters, while Short offers four 10 minute periods. Make your choice between the two game clocks at the first screen, using the up or down arrows. Press the Start button to begin the game.

SCORING POINTS

Just like real football, you earn 6 points for a touchdown, 3 points for a field goal and points after touchdown are worth 1 point. If you can trap the opponent in his own end zone, you will score a safety, worth 2 points.

OFFENSE

When you have the ball, your first duty will be to select an offensive play.

To select a play, press the Up or Down arrow key to move the cursor to CHANGE and then press the **A button.** Now press the Down arrow to review your available options. You will see on your screen a display that includes the current score, the remaining time in the quarter, the current quarter, the location of the ball, the number of downs used and the number of yards remaining to the next first down.

At the top of the Offensive Play Selection Screen you will see a diagram of the available offensive plays. All 11 players are shown on the screen, with arrows indicating the direction they are supposed to go once the ball is in play. You'll want to pay particular attention to the players marked "A" and "B". These are the primary receivers for the play that will be put into motion if the currently shown play is selected. The position of the quarterback at the start of play is shown by a half-black circle.

The available offensive plays are:

Shot Gun. A formation used mostly as a setup for passing in which the quarterback stands a few yards behind the center to receive a direct snap, with the other backs spread out as flankers and slotbacks.

T Formation. A formation in which the quarterback lines up close behind the center with the fullback about 4 to 5 yards behind him and the halfbacks on either side of and slightly ahead of the fullback, giving the appearance of a T.

Slot T. A variation of the T Formation in which the tight end is spread away from the tackle and the flankerback moves over to a position behind the slot between the tackle and tight end or split end.

Pro T. A variation of the T Formation in which the two running backs are behind the quarterback and the other back is wide as a flanker.

Y Formation. Also known as the "Wishbone" or "Wishbone T" formation, this pattern has replaced the T and I setups for many pro teams. The halfbacks are lined up farther from the line of scrimmage than is the fullback; the appearance of the four backs (QB, FB and HB) gives the appearance of a wishbone from above.

I Formation. A formation in which the set backs line up directly behind the quarterback.

When you are showing on the screen the play you wish to use, press the **A button.** The screen will now change to the lineup. Your quarterback (and the location of the ball) will be indicated with an arrow marked "1", while the primary defensive player will be marked with a "2" arrow. Press the **A button** to snap the ball (if you delay too long to snap the ball, the computer will do it for you). Now you will be able to watch as a player marked "A" and a player marked "B" move down the field.

Move your quarterback as necessary in the backfield, and then press the **A or B button** to throw the ball to either of those eligible receivers. Be careful, though: if you throw into a thicket of players, the ball is likely to be intercepted. If the ball is caught by one of your receivers, the "1" arrow will move to mark their current location as they move down the field in hopes of scoring a touchdown.

Your other option is to "bootleg" the ball and run with it yourself. This is a lot safer than throwing the ball blindly, and in certain circumstances you may be able to pick up a down, yardage or even a touchdown this way.

If there is an interception or fumble, a new arrow will appear above the defensive player who has stolen the ball, and you will be forced into a defensive situation.

PUNTING

You also are given the option to Punt the ball. This can be done at any time, but in general (and especially in this computer simulation) you will want to reserve this play for times when you are on your fourth down with long yardage, or when you are hopelessly trapped deep in your own territory.

FIELD GOALS

Any time you have advanced to within your opponent's 40-yard line, the punt option will be replaced by a Field Goal choice. Select the option and press the **A button** when the ball has been snapped to your kicker.

DEFENSE

When it is your turn to defend against a touchdown, you will control the player with the arrow above his head.

There are seven available defensive patterns. Six of them are indicated by a number: the first number tells how many players are positioned on the line of scrimmage; the second number tells how many players are on a secondary line, and so on.

When you believe the other team will try a passing play, for example, you may want to have more players back from the line so they can maneuver to intercept the pass. If you anticipate a running play you might place more people on the line to block the running advance.

A 5-2 defense means five players on the line, two behind them, and the rest of the team positioned however seems best for a given situation. In other words, in a 5-2 defense only seven positions are defined, the rest vary with the current game situation.

Here are the available defenses:

5-2
5-3-3
3-5-3
4-3-4
4-4-3
6-2
Goal Line

The Goal Line defense is a special defense intended to block any movement at all of the ball in situations where the opposing team is at or near the goal line. In the Game Boy NFL game, the Goal Line Defense is a 7-3-1 pattern, with seven defenders positioned on the line of scrimmage, three backs spread behind them and one safety positioned further back.

When you see the display of available defenses, hit the Down arrow to go through them one by one until you find the pattern you want to use. Press the **A button** to lock it in.

At this point, control of the ball is in the "hands" of your computer or human opponent. In the few seconds before the ball is snapped, you can call a defense "audible" that changes the player you will control. Press the **A or B buttons** until the player you want to run with is under the arrow; once the ball is snapped, the specified player will be in command.

NFL is a registered trademark of the National Football League. Team names and logos are the registered trademarks of NFL and the teams depicted. Konami is a registered trademark of Konami Inc. Game pak © 1990 Konami Inc.

Tennis

AGE: 6 to Adult
DIFFICULTY: Apprentice-Hot Dog

Tennis looks so easy from the grandstands, but it is a lot harder to play. Tennis, the new Game Boy game pak, looks easy, too. But it requires every bit as much concentration, anticipation and reflex responses as the real thing.

To tell the truth, we had our doubts when we plugged this one into the slot. It sounded too much like the old, dull Pong game from back in the ancient history of video games. In Pong, you moved a large paddle up and down to hit a ball across a line. Yawn.

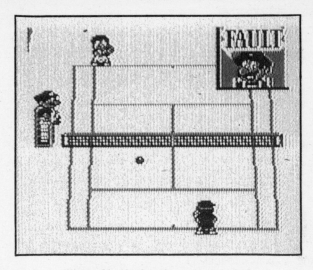

The ref looks familiar, doesn' t he?

There's a fair amount of Pong in Tennis, although you do have quite a bit more control over play. You can place your serves, lob or smash your returns, charge the net and choose between forehand or backhand play. You can play against the tough computer opponent (selecting from four levels of difficulty) or you can hook up two Game Boys for head-to-head competition.

It is the Video Link game that makes this Tennis stand out from the rest of the pack of sports games.

And there is this vaguely familiar umpire who calls faults and keeps score. Where have we seen this guy before?

About Tennis

Tennis is one of the world's most popular sporting games. It is played by more than 20 million Americans on one level or another, and perhaps twice that many people worldwide.

The word tennis is derived from the Old French name for the game, tenetz. According to historians, a game something like tennis was played in late-13th-century France among the upper classes. The Italians and the Greeks played a similar game during that period. The French game was called jeu de paume ("game of the palm") because the players used the palms of their hands to strike the ball. Racquets were added later to give players greater reach.

Changing sides after completion of a set.

The game came to America in 1874 in the baggage of Mary Ewing Outerbridge, a wealthy woman from Staten Island, New York who came across the game while on vacation in Bermuda.

MANUFACTURER: Nintendo

NUMBER OF PLAYERS
1 or 2. 2-player requires second Game Boy and Video Link cable.

CHARACTERS
Mario is the umpire, and you get to play better tennis than most of us have ever hoped for.

STARTING THE GAME
From the title screen, you can choose 1-player or 2-player games. You can only select 2-player if there are two Game Boy devices connected with Video Link cables, each with its own copy of the Tennis game.

You can also choose to turn off the music and play with just the sound effects of the tennis game.

CONTROL PAD
Arrows: Move the player left or right and back and forth on the court. Also control placement of the ball when hit.

On Serves, Strokes or Smashes, the arrow keys can be used to affect the distance and placement of the ball. Press the Up, Down, Left or Right arrow as you press the **A or B buttons** in the game, as follows:

Left Arrow directs the serve or stroke to the left side of the court.

Right Arrow directs the serve or stroke to the right side of the court.

Up Arrow directs the ball deep into the opposing court.

Down Arrow directs the ball on a shorter path into the opposing court.

Practice your timing. If the arrow key is pressed before the **A or B button,** the player will move before he swings, and you will miss the ball. Press the **A or B button** and then the arrow key for a directed shot.

"A" BUTTON:

SERVICE: Press the **A button** to toss the tennis ball up in the air. Press the **A button** again to hit the ball hard. See the note under Arrows for ways to direct the flight of the ball.

STROKE (VOLLEY): Press the **A button** to hit the ball hard.

SMASH: When the ball is hit with the tennis racket above the player's head, the stroke becomes a downward smash. Press the **A button** to hit the ball hard.

"B" BUTTON:

SERVICE: When the ball has been tossed, press the **B button** to hit the ball more slowly. See the note under Arrows for ways to direct the flight of the ball.

STROKE (VOLLEY): Press the **B button** to hit the ball weakly. When you hit the ball from deep in your own end, this will result in a "lob," a high, easy shot that is harder to return than it might seem. A lob is particularly effective if your opponent has charged the net; just pop the ball over his head.

SMASH: When the ball is hit with the tennis racket above the player's head, the stroke becomes a downward smash. Press the **B button** to hit the ball weakly.

PAUSE

To call a time out in the game, press the **Start** button; press the button again to resume play. While the game is paused, you can also press the **Select** button to see a display of the current score and status of the game. Each time you press **Select** another element of the score will be shown. The information, in the order shown on the screen, is:

Point Display. What you will see is something like this:

C = 40
P = 15

which means that the Computer has 40 points and the Player has 15. See the note on tennis scoring below.

Set/Game Display. You'll see a report on where in the match you are, as in:

SET
2
GAME
5

which means that you are in the second set (of three in the match) and are playing the fifth game (you must win six games [seven in the case of a tie at 5–5] to win a match).

Count. Here you'll learn the results of each set played thus far, as in:

	1	2	3
P	6	2	0
C	4	3	0

which means that the Player won the first set by a score of 6–4 games, but is trailing in the second set by a score of 2–3 to the Computer.

Match/Level. This display reminds you of the type of game you have selected, indicating the number of sets in the match and the level of play selected.

NUMBER OF LEVELS

4. The higher the game level, the faster the player will be able to run, but the ball moves faster, too.

NUMBER OF GAMES

The standard competition is made up of 6 games per set, with the winner of 2 out of 3 sets the winner of the match.

If you would prefer to play a 1-set match, hold down the **A button** when you press **Start**.

2-PLAYER GAME

An exciting variation of the Tennis game pak comes when you hook up two Game Boys for head-to-head competition over the Video Link cable. In addition to a second Game Boy, you'll need two Tennis game paks and the cable. As with all Video Link games, connect the cable and install the game paks with the power OFF and then turn both machines on.

In the game, each player will see the game from his or her perspective. In other words, when you a receiving a serve you will see your opponent toss the ball and hit it toward you; at the same time, your opponent will see you maneuver into position to return the serve.

The first player to select the 2-player game will serve first.

SCORING

The competition is divided into games, sets and the match. You must win six games to win a set; you must win two out of three sets to win the match.

Scoring in tennis is not that difficult to understand, although it is not particularly logical in its progression. The winner of each volley wins a "point; the player who gets 4 points first wins the game, except if the players are tied at 3 points apiece, in which case the game continues until one player scores two points in a row.

The actual recording of points is done like this:

0 (called "Love" at the start of the game. One explanation for the use of the word "love" is that it is descended from the French word "l'oeuf," meaning "the egg," or zero.

15 First point.

30 Second point.

40 Third point.

If the two players are tied at 40–40 (3 points apiece, it is called "deuce," also from the French, and meaning "twos."

The first player to win 6 games wins a set, unless the opponents are tied at 5 games apiece. If that happens, the set goes to 7 games. If the two players tie again at 6 games apiece, there will be a one-game tiebreaker. The tiebreaking game is awarded to the player who is first to score 7 points; if the players tie at 6 points each in the tiebreaker, the first player to win two consecutive points is awarded the set.

THE RULES

Your ball must land within the "chalk" lines indicated on the screen in your opponent's court. If your ball goes out of bounds, Umpire Mario will declare it "Out."

When you serve, you must hit the ball from behind your service line into the receive serve area of your opponent, diagonally across the court. If the ball does not land in the service area, Umpire Mario will declare a

"Fault." You are allowed only one fault per serve; a second fault will cost you a point. If your service hits the net and continues into the opponent's service area, it is called a "Let" and the serve must be done over without penalty. If the ball hits the net and does not go over, or lands outside of the service area, it is a "Fault."

At the completion of each odd-numbered game (1, 3 and 5 in most sets) the players change sides.

POWER PLAYER HINTS

Just as in real tennis, if you fault on your first service, you should go for a safe second serve. Just keep your finger off the arrow keys and use the **A button** to toss the ball and the **B button** to hit it for a safe and predictable serve.

Tennis © 1989 Nintendo of America Inc.

World Bowling

AGE: 6 years-Adult
DIFFICULTY: Novice-Apprentice

MANUFACTURER: Romstar / (213) 539-5283

NUMBER OF PLAYERS

1 or 2 bowlers.

CHARACTERS

You are Boy or Girl. What could be simpler? Well, actually, if you want to you can have Boy #1 and Boy #2 or Girl #1 and Girl #2 in a 2-player match, or you can mix the sexes.

What's the difference between the bowlers? Well, Boy is right-handed (even though he raises his left hand in the title screen) and Girl is left-handed (but raises her right hand). Beyond that, their abilities seem equal.

CONTROL PAD:

Arrows: Use the control pad to move the player Left or Right into position on the screen. You can see where you line up in the overhead

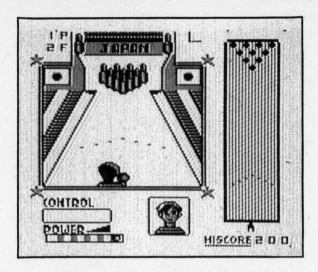

Early in the game, on the Japanese lanes.

display of the alleyway on the right side of the screen. Press the **A button** to lock your bowler into position.

"A" BUTTON:

> *HOOK CONTROL:* Once the player is in position, the indicator in the Control Bar section at the bottom of the screen will begin to move left and right. Depending on where the indicator is when you press the **A button,** the ball will go straight or hook to the left or right. If the indicator is to the left, the ball will hook to the left; if the indicator is to the right of center, the ball will hook to the right. If you freeze the indicator in the center, the ball will be released straight down the alley.

> *POWER CONTROL:* Next you must select the amount of power to be applied to the ball. The indicator in the Power Bar will move right and left. The further the indicator is to the right, the more power will be applied. Press the **A button** to lock in your choice and release the ball.

"B" BUTTON: Displays the current scorecard. Press the **B button** again to resume play.

NUMBER OF WORLDS

You'll be able to visit bowling alleys in six countries along the way. The screen display includes the qualifying score you will need to earn in order to advance to the next round:

Japan	200
China	210
U.S.	220
Canada	230
France	240
England	250

But, hey, this is bowling. Each lane looks like any other, except that you'll see the flag of the nation you are visiting on the screen, and there is a different musical soundtrack for each location. Finally, you'll find a pair of different mascots for each country: a dancer or animal to celebrate a strike and a tormentor to pick on you for a gutter ball.

The various bowling lanes are different, though. Each country's alleys have slightly different characteristics, including "tracks" that are worn into the wood. Some of the alleys may favor a leftie over a rightie, or vice versa.

In the one-player game, you will always start in Japan; in the two-player version you can select your starting point.

NUMBER OF LEVELS

There are no choices of level in the game, but you can choose the weight of the ball you wish to throw, between a minimum of 7 pounds and a maximum of 15. The heavier ball has more firepower when it hits, of course, but is somewhat harder to control.

SCORING POINTS

World Bowling follows the standard rules and scoring practices of a scratch bowling match, with score based on total pin count.

Each game is divided into 10 frames, each of which allows two attempts to knock down the 10 pins. If all 10 pins are knocked down with the first ball thrown, it is called a Strike; if all 10 pins are knocked down by the combination of the first and second ball thrown, it is called a Spare. For a Strike, the bowler would receive for that frame 10 points plus the total number of pins knocked down with the next two balls he throws; for a Spare, the bowler would receive 10 points plus the total number of pins knocked down with the next ball thrown.

If a strike or spare is rolled in the 10th frame, a total of 3 balls can be thrown after then to determine the bonus. The highest possible score in bowling, received for 12 consecutive strikes, is 300.

The scorecard produced by World Bowling uses a diagonal slash to indicate a spare, an X for a strike, a dash for a miss and a G to indicate a gutterball—a thrown ball that misses everything and ends up in one of the gutters along the side of the alley.

POWER PLAYER HINTS

It is actually most difficult to knock down all 10 pins with a straight-in throw. You will likely score more strikes taking advantage of a hook.

Remember, too, to take into account the right- or left-handedness of your bowler. For a right-handed bowler, a perfect hooked strike may be thrown by launching the ball slightly to the right of the front pin and hooking it into the left. For a left-handed bowler, the technique is reversed—launch the ball at a spot slightly to the left of the front pin, with the ball hooking to the right.

·||·
21 Sneak Peeks

·5·
Game Boy Previews

The process of creating, designing, programming and marketing a Game Boy game can take a year or more from first idea to first copy in the store. As we completed this book, we could see more than 40 additional games that were in progress. We'll tell you what we know about some of them now.

Turtles in Your Hand

Pass the pizza please. Look for those wacky Teenage Mutant Ninja Turtles in an all-new Game Boy adventure called the *Fall of the Foot Clan* from Ultra Software.

"From the depths of New York sewers to the bowels of the Game Boy come your favorite heroes in a half shell, primed for an all-new defense of life, liberty and the pursuit of pizza," the designers say.

Your fingers on the Game Boy control the Turtles' every karate chop, Katana slice and pizza munch as Raphael, Donatello, Michelangelo and Leonardo bust up five of Manhattan's most scenic locations, including Chump Tower, Taxi Jam and Waste Dump Ravine.

Dedicated Turtle-holics can play a scaled-down dedicated version of the Ninja challenge; you can read about the game in the special section on handheld games in this book.

Wizards and Warriors

A Battle on the bridge.

Kuros, the gallant knight warrior, returns for another bout of gallantry, this time in the palm of your hand. *Wizards and Warriors X: The Fortress of Fear* is due from Acclaim.

Kuros will leap through castle ruins, travel on clouds and battle dozens of deadly characters, from flying two-headed eagles and giant bats to slithering serpent beasts.

We bet you veteran NES game players thought you had gotten rid of Wizard Malkil at the end of the first Wizards & Warrior game! (You did make it all the way to the end, didn't you?)

Well, you were wrong. He's back, and this time he has taken control of the forces of nature: earth, wind, water and fire. Within each of these four domains, you'll fight off another dizzying set of monsters and perils. You'll be able to ask for the help of an Animal King, but he'll respond only if you are able to pay him with the golden object he is looking for. At the end of each domain, you'll have the privilege of facing the Elemental itself.

You'll need to collect as much magic as you can to beat the Elementals; with each victory, you'll obtain a piece of the shattered IronSword, which you will need in your final battle, this one against old Malkil himself at the top of the strange IceFire Mountain.

You will also find a dedicated handheld game version of the Wizards and Warriors series, also from Acclaim. You can read about this much simpler game in the special section about handheld games in Part 3 of this book.

Wrasslin'

Try not to grunt too much.

A different kind of fighting will be on your hands with the release of *WWF Superstars* in a Game Boy version, from Acclaim. Included in the cartridge are eight of the World Wrestling Federation's biggest stars, including Hulk Hogan, The Ultimate Warrior and "Macho Man" Randy Savage.

There is already on the market a Nintendo Entertainment System game pak called WWF Wrestlemania where you can live out your weirdest fantasies and become Hulk Hogan or Randy "Macho Man" Savage or even Andre the Giant.

In the NES version, each of the wrestlers has different moves assigned to different buttons and button combinations. Reading, and keeping handy, the instruction manual is a must here.

Short Takes

Unless the people from Seika can come up with a better name, look for a challenging maze game called *Heart Attack*. Relentless deathballs strike at random while you try to stay on course and maneuver through the landscapes of ever-changing barriers. There are 50 levels of escalating jeopardy.

LJN also plans to bring over some of its other big hits to the Game Boy, including *Beetlejuice*, *Town & Country Surf Designs* and *NBA Basketball*.

Under the Beautiful Sea

Power Mission takes your Game Boy below the waves in a submarine warfare simulation from NTVIC.

Power Mission simulates a deep sea battle against a powerful enemy force. You begin by selecting and deploying your own fleet, from a group of seven. Next you use your onboard radar to track down the enemy. And, finally, launch your attack with missiles and other naval weapons.

There are 10 stages in Power Mission. As you clear each level, the enemy fleet will gain more and more power. The goal of the game is simple: the fighter that sinks his opponent's fleet first wins.

The game can be played by one or two players, and includes a password feature to continue play. The designers of this game have squeezed a great deal of detail into the screens.

Big Sports, Little Game

You'll get a kick out of this one: *Soccer-Mania* from CSG Imagesoft is a nice translation to the Game Boy screen. This game really is a ball when two players use a Video Link for a head-to-head (ouch!) competition.

The wizards have managed to squeeze two of sports' biggest (and we mean big) stars into a tiny Game Boy cartridge in *Jordan vs. Bird: One on One*, due from Milton Bradley near the end of 1990.

The game stars Larry Bird and Michael Jordan in three games: play against a friend or the computer as Bird or Jordan; enter a slam dunk contest with Jordan and join Bird in a 3-point shoot-out.

A Better Mousetrap

Move over Minnie, Mickey and Mighty: here's Maxie Mouse in the adventure of *Mousetrap Hotel*, due out from Milton Bradley near the end of 1990.

"Help Maxie Mouse make his way from the basement to his posh luxury mousehole in the penthouse! Along the way be ready to deal with bad-tempered blind mice, laundry chutes, army ants, maids with deadly vacuum cleaners and all kinds of really nasty mousetraps! Each room Maxie passes through has its own unique pitfalls and challenges. When Maxie eats cheese, see how his tail transforms into all kinds of useful tools."

How Do You Spell Game Boy?

We're really intrigued by this one: a version of the classic board game Scrabble available in a handheld electronic game. It's called, logically enough, *Super Scrabble*, and it will be offered by Milton Bradley near the end of the year.

They've included all of the basic elements of Scrabble, and added a few special features including sound effects. You can compete against the computer, or against a friend on ten different skill levels.

The screen displays the board as well as your letter rack, score panel and a clock to keep track of time limits. And, in case you have a question about the spelling of an entry, you can consult the program's built-in 30,000 word dictionary.

Teases

Electro Brain was scrambling to finish—and win Nintendo approval—for a new game called *Dead Heat Scramble*, a demolition derby/race that takes place inside a half-tube. Think of it as the skateboarding portion of California Games using cars instead of rollerboards and you'll get the idea. Just to make it even more interesting, Dead Heat Scramble can also be played by two contestants using Video Link-ed Game Boys.

Watch for the fall 1990 arrival of *Burai Fighter Deluxe*, a portable version of the fearsome Burai Fighter outerspace shoot-em-up from Taxan. And look for a handheld version of the hugely popular *Double Dragon* from Tradewest near the end of 1990.

Bullet Proof Software will bring Game Boy versions of its new *Hatris* and *Pipe Dream* games in the fall.

We took a look at some of the very early plans for the Pipe Dream game. Here's some of the story line:

"Can you think under pressure? How about under flooz pressure.
You'll find out when you play Pipe Dream, the fast-flowing game of
speed, strategy and plumbing. Make your pipeline as long as you can,
but always stay ahead of the flow or your score will go down the
drain."

The game will present about 36 increasingly difficult levels. The opening
screen is empty except for a starting piece. You can place a pipe of various
shapes anywhere on the screen you would like; the object is to connect
everything together before the flooz has flowed.

The Great Warrior SAGA is the working title for a new role-playing game
for the Game Boy from Square Soft. The game is a journey through four
worlds to save Paradise from the ravages of the evil Ashuras (Devils)

Watch for *Ultima* on the Game Boy some time in 1990, from FCI.

Also due by the summer from Ultra is *Bill Elliott's Nascar Fast Tracks*
(although the title may change).

Heiankyo Alien, from Meldac, is another "Dig the holes to trap the
invading aliens before they take over your friendly village game."

Vic Tokai is readying *Daedalian Opus,* vaguely related to Tetris. You'll
have to twist and turn geometric shapes so they will fit into the openings on
the puzzle. The farther you go, the harder they come.

·III·
Special Handheld Games

·6·
Acclaim
Entertainment

If you are a *true* Teenage Mutant Ninja Turtles fan, or a dyed-in-the-wool Skate or Die follower or an incurable Hulkamaniac your collection may not be complete. Many of the same games that are big hits in Nintendo and Game Boy versions are also available in simplified handheld toy versions.

We do need to point out that the game play and depth of these inexpensive games are considerably less than those of their Game Boy cousins, but they are nevertheless fun. We've chosen 12 of the most popular handheld games from two manufacturers, Acclaim and Konami, for inclusion in this special section. We've divided the games into groups according to their manufacturer, because each handheld is of a different design.

1943: The Battle of Midway

Aw, shoot: here come enemy bombers, enemy destroyers and enemy tornadoes. Enemy tornadoes?

You're at the controls of your own P-38 fighter plane in one of the pivotal battles of World War II. You must fly five missions, each more difficult than the one before. There are two levels of difficulty.

MANUFACTURER: Acclaim

CHARACTERS: Just you against them.

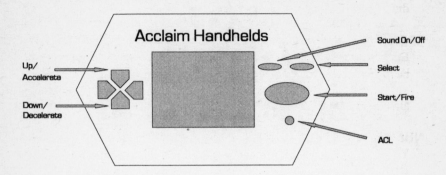

CONTROL PAD

Arrow: Moves your P-38 Up, Down, Left or Right. Your plane will move from one row to another in even jumps.

Select: Press the button once to choose the Level 1 (Beginner) or Level 2 (Advanced) game. You will see "L-1" or "L-2" displayed on the screen.

Start/Fire: Starts the game, fires the machine guns and restarts the game in the Continue mode.

You can only fire at planes when you are in the top three positions. You can only fire at boats when you are in the bottom three positions.

Sound On/Off: Press the button to turn the sound off; press the button again to resume the din.

Reset: If the game malfunctions, press the tiny ACL button with the tip of a pen or a toothpick. Pressing this button will also erase the electronic record of the previous high score. Note that the game will likely begin to act unpredictably as battery power runs out.

NUMBER OF STAGES

There are five stages to complete:

Stage 1. Shoot the planes.

Stage 2. Shoot the planes and avoid the tornadoes. There's a 1,000 point bonus for completion of the stage.

Stage 3. Avoid the planes and shoot the boats.

Stage 4. Avoid the planes and the tornadoes. Pick up the 1,000-point bonus for completion of the stage.

Stage 5. Shoot the planes and avoid the tornadoes.

In case this all sounds too complicated, just remember this: shoot and duck, duck and shoot.

SPECIAL!

Enemy planes that come at you from the left side of the screen cannot be destroyed by your machine guns! Avoid them at all costs.

You also cannot destroy oncoming tornadoes, but we guess you already know that.

NUMBER OF LIVES

You start the game with three lives. You can earn a free life for each 10,000 points scored.

ON/OFF

There is no on/off switch for the game. Instead, the game will automatically turn itself off three or four minutes after the last button has been pushed.

If you are going to be putting your game away for a few months, it would probably be best to remove the batteries to eliminate the possibility of leakage.

Removing or replacing the batteries will erase the record of the highest score.

SCORING POINTS

You'll win 100 points for each enemy fighter plane, bomber or naval destroyer you remove from the battle.

There is a 1,000-point bonus for destroying 3 planes or boats lined up in a row. (You'll also receive the base 300 points.)

And, there is a special 1,000-point bonus for completing stages 2 and 4.

The highest score that can be displayed is 99,900 points. If you're **that** good, the scoreboard will return to 0, but the last two zeros on the screen will continue to flash, allowing you to rack up a score as high as 199,800 points, which is more than we can reasonably hope for.

POWER ZOOMING

There are unlimited Continues, allowing you to resume play at the start of the level you were in when the game ended, although your score will be reset to 0.

A BIT OF HISTORY

For those of you who are history buffs, here's a little background about the Battle of Midway, which actually took place in 1942.

Midway Island is really two tiny islands located 1,300 miles northwest of Honolulu in the Pacific Ocean. It was discovered by the United States in 1859 and annexed in 1867. It is still a territory of the United States, controlled by the U.S. Navy.

The Battle of Midway occurred June 4–7, 1942 and was Japan's first major defeat of the war. It crippled Japan's naval air power and ended Japan's attempt to seize Midway as a base from which to strike Hawaii.

The Japanese Admiral Yamamoto had a larger fleet. However, unbeknownst to Japan, the Americans had cracked Japan's secret codes, enabling American Admiral Chester Nimitz to know about Yamamoto's plans in advance.

On June 4, 1942, aircraft from the 100-ship Japanese fleet began blasting Midway. Nimitz' task-force commanders launched aircraft from the carriers Enterprise, Hornet and Yorktown. At the end of the two-day battle, Japan had lost four carriers and a major part of its air arm. Japanese submarines did succeed in sinking the Yorktown.

The P-38 fighter of the American forces was called "Lightning." It was a strange looking bird, with the single pilot sitting between two straight booms that each held a large engine. The fuselage was long, with a protruding nose in front of the pilot, but the midsection was clipped sharply behind the pilot.

The real P-38 had a wingspan of 52 feet, was 37 feet long and weighed about 20,000 pounds. Its two 1,385-horsepower engines allowed it a maximum speed of 395 mph with a range of 425 miles. The highest it could fly was 39,000 feet. It was armed with one 20-mm cannon, four machine guns and about a ton of bombs.

Combat Zone

Boom, boom, sheboom. You've got a bazooka and a lot of nerve in this game. On the tiny screen come wave after wave of enemy soldiers, bomb-dropping helicopters and tanks. On the ground are munitions stores.

You use the control keys to move an onscreen bazooka sight; when it is near a target, press the Fire button. That's about it. The action gets faster and furiouser the deeper into the three levels you go. And watch carefully: if the soldier is carrying a gun, he's a threat, but if he's carrying a white flag, he's on your side and it is considered bad sport to shoot him.

MANUFACTURER: Acclaim Entertainment

CHARACTERS

It's you, super commando, in an unidentified Combat Zone, fighting everything (well, almost everything) that moves. We have no idea where you are, although the opening musical flourish is the Marseillaise, the national anthem of France. (*Allons enfants de la patrie, le jour de gloire est arrivé*): Come children of the homeland, the day of glory has arrived.) Let's pretend we're in the French Foreign Legion.

CONTROL PAD

Arrows: The arrows are used to aim your bazooka sight to the Left, Right, Up or Down.

Select: Used to choose skill levels or the Demo mode, or to enter the Continue mode.

Start/Fire: Starts the game, fires the bazooka and restarts the game in the Continue mode.

Sound On/Off: Press the button to turn off the sound effects and music; press the button again to restore the clatter.

Reset: If the game malfunctions, press the tiny ACL button with the tip of a pen or a toothpick. Pressing this button will also erase the electronic record of the previous high score. Note that the game will likely begin to act unpredictably as battery power runs out.

NUMBER OF WORLDS: There are three missions in the game.

NUMBER OF LIVES

You have just one life to lose. The game will start with six Power Units displayed in the upper right corner of the screen; when all six have been lost, the game is over. You can restore a life unit by destroying a fully loaded Power Station.

ON/OFF

There is no on/off switch for the game. Instead, the game will automatically turn itself off three or four minutes after the last button has been pushed.

If you are going to be putting your game away for a few months, it would probably be best to remove the batteries to eliminate the possibility of leakage.

Removing or replacing the batteries will erase the record of the highest score.

SCORING POINTS

Enemy Soldier.	
Dynamite Bomb.	100 points.
Helicopter.	
Tank.	200 points.
Power Station when you have 5 or fewer Power Units remaining.	1 Power unit.
Power Station when you have a full set of 6 Power Units.	500 points.

You'll lose points for the following:

Shooting soldier with flag.	Lose 100 points.
Allowing dynamite to reach the ground when dropped by copter.	Lose 1 Power unit.
Being shot by enemy soldier.	Lose 1 Power unit.

The maximum score that can be displayed on the screen is 99,900 points. If you get past that score (really?) the scoreboard will return to 0 and the last two zeros will flash continuously, allowing you the chance to score a total of 199,800 points.

CONTINUE

The game includes an arcade-style continue mode, allowing you to continue as many times as you want, each time returning to the start of the level you were in at the time the game ended.

When the game ends, press the Select button to continue the game.

If you press the Start button, you will resume play at the last round you reached in the game just ended, with a score of 0.

If you press the Select button again to exit the Continue mode, you can start over again (press Select again to change to skill level L1 or L2) and then press Start.

Knight Rider

This is a handheld game based on the Nintendo video game that was based on the television series of several years ago. As a matter of fact, come to think of it the television series was kind of like a video game.

The two stars of the game are Michael Knight and his supercar, KITT. Knight was born as Michael Long and was a promising young detective. But while out on a case, he was shot down by a gang of international criminals. Along comes Wilton Knight, the mysterious founder of the mysterious Knight Foundation, who mysteriously brings Michael back to life as his adopted stepson. He gives Michael the keys to the family car, KITT.

But don't worry much about the story line. Just drive.

The goal of this game is to reach five big-city checkpoints along the way in your cross-country battle against an international crime ring. To reach each checkpoint, you will have to make your way through four challenges.

Keep an eye out for the specially marked trailer trucks of the Knight Rider Foundation; they're stocked with resupplies!

MANUFACTURER: Acclaim Entertainment, Inc.

CHARACTERS
You are Michael Knight, and your car is named KITT.

CONTROL PAD
Arrows: The Left and Right arrows move KITT in those directions.
The Up arrow is the accelerator; the Down arrow the brake. Press the brake several times to bring the car to a full stop.

Select: Press the button once to choose Level 1 (Beginner), or twice to choose Level 2 (Advanced).

Start/Fire: Fires KITT's missiles. Starts the game and restarts the game in the Continue mode.

Sound On/Off: Press the button once to turn off the music and sound effects; press the button again to restore the racket.

Reset: If the game malfunctions, press the tiny ACL button with the tip of a pen or a toothpick. Pressing this button will also erase the electronic record of the previous high score. Note that the game will likely begin to act unpredictably as battery power runs out.

TIMING

You will have only a limited amount of time to complete each stage; when you are about to go off the clock, the VICTORY sign will flash and a warning tone will sound.

NUMBER OF WORLDS

There are five checkpoints to be reached; you'll need to go through four stages to get to each checkpoints, for a total of 20 challenges.

NUMBER OF LIVES

The game is over when the enemy lands four hits. You can keep track of your damage by consulting the meter at the bottom left corner of the screen.

ON/OFF

There is no on/off switch for the game. Instead, the game will automatically turn itself off three or four minutes after the last button has been pushed.

If you are going to be putting your game away for a few months, it would probably be best to remove the batteries to eliminate the possibility of leakage.

Removing or replacing the batteries will erase the record of the highest score.

SCORING POINTS

Destroying an Armed Car.   100 points

Destroying Enemy Aircraft.   200 points

Failure to Complete Stage
in the allowed time.   Lose 100 points.

When you get past a checkpoint, it will be marked off on the tiny map displayed in the upper right corner of the screen.

The maximum score that can be displayed on the screen is 99,900 points. If you get past that score (really?) the scoreboard will return to 0 and the last two zeros will flash continuously, allowing you the chance to score a total of 199,800 points.

CONTINUE

The game includes an arcade-style Continue mode, allowing you to continue as many times as you want, each time returning to the start of the level you were in at the time the game ended.

When the game ends, press the Select button to continue the game.

If you press the Start button, you will resume play at the last round you reached in the game just ended, with a score of 0.

If you press the Select button again to exit the Continue mode, you can start over again (press Select again to change to skill level L1 or L2) and then press Start.

Ring King

Boxing is an awful lot safer when all you've got to throw are your thumbs. That explains the success of Punch Out! and Ring King in their various arcade and full-sized Nintendo Entertainment System versions.

Here is a scaled-down version of Ring King, available in a dedicated handheld version from Acclaim. Included are four different mini-challenges: three rounds of training and one bout, conducted at a Lightweight, Middleweight or Heavyweight level.

The three preliminary rounds of training serve to build up the power of your fighter before he gets into the ring with a real opponent.

MANUFACTURER: Acclaim Entertainment

CHARACTERS
You're the Champ, entering the ring with a modestly successful lifetime record of 53-0.

CONTROL PAD
Arrows: The Left arrow moves your fighter forward; the Right arrow moves him backward. The Up arrow makes him jump; the Down arrow makes him duck or dodge a punch.

Select: Used to select a Light, Middle or Heavyweight championship bout.

Start/Punch: Press to start the game with the first of three training rounds.

Once a round is underway, press the Punch button to throw a punch.

Sound On/Off: Press the button to turn off the sound effects and music; press the button again to resume the noise.

Reset: If the game malfunctions, press the tiny ACL button with the tip of a pen or a toothpick. Pressing this button will also erase the electronic record of the previous high score. Note that the game will likely begin to act unpredictably as battery power runs out.

NUMBER OF COMPETITIONS

You'll start out the competition with a series of three rounds of training. Your purpose here should be to get into mental and physical shape for the upcoming fight, as well as building up power points for the bout. Power earned in each of the training rounds is retained into the next round.

Training Round 1: The Sandbag

Punch the heavy training bag in the middle of its swing as many times as you can in the time limit. Every 20 punches is worth 1 power unit. Each time you're hit by the swinging bag, though, you'll lose power.

Press the Punch button to throw a punch; press the Down arrow to dodge the swinging bag.

Training Round 2: Agility Training

You're in a small room with a bunch of bouncing balls heading at your body and head. Punch or dodge out of the way of the oncoming balls. Each 10 balls you avoid or hit will earn you 1 power unit. Each time you are hit by one of the ball, you will lose some power.

Training Round 3: Contact Sparring

This is a friendly partner in the ring with you. He'll move his glove up or down to present a target. Punch at it as many times as you can in the time available. Every 20 punches landed is worth 1 power unit; missed punches will cost you power.

Punch. Straight punch.

Punch and Jump together. Uppercut.

Punch and Dodge together. Lower body blow.

Championship Match

Each level—Lightweight, Middleweight or Heavyweight—presents three matches. If you win the first fight, you will go back through the training rounds again to build some more power before you face a stronger opponent. If you manage to win 3 fights in a row, you will be crowned the undefeated Ring King.

You'll see on the display your opponent's points (left of the : mark) and your points (to the right of the :). At the right side of the screen you'll see a graphic showing the remaining time in the match.

If you are knocked down, you must press the Jump (Up arrow) button before the 10-count ends, or the referee will declare a KO. You will not be able to stand up if you have no remaining power.

The game goes to the fighter who scores the most points in a match or a KO.

Punch. Straight punch.

Punch and Jump together. Uppercut.

Punch and Dodge together. Lower body blow.

Backward. Used to backpedal away from your opponent.

Jump. Allows you to stand up after a knockdown, if you have power.

ON/OFF

There is no on/off switch for the game. Instead, the game will automatically turn itself off three or four minutes after the last button has been pushed.

If you are going to be putting your game away for a few months, it would probably be best to remove the batteries to eliminate the possibility of leakage.

Removing or replacing the batteries will erase the record of the highest score.

Wizards & Warriors: The Ultimate Warrior vs. the Evil Wizard

It's still the same old story, a fight for love and glory, a case of do or die.

Yes, welcome back Kuros, the Knight Warrior. Your assignment is to rescue the princess (what, again?) and defeat the evil wizard (didn't we do that last time?)

Right here in your hand, you'll battle giant spiders, killer bees and deadly fireballs. Use your sword to destroy fearsome bats and eventually Malkil himself. Collect diamonds for bonus points and the magic keys to open the castle gate.

Game play is pretty good, although it is not near the response of the Game Boy or the full-sized NES machine.

MANUFACTURER: Acclaim

CHARACTERS:

You are Kuros, the Knight Warrior, out for battle to the end against Malkil and his minions.

CONTROL PAD

Arrows: Use the Left or Right arrows to move in those directions.

Use the Up arrow to Jump, to avoid fire balls, grab diamonds and keys and in combination with the Attack button.

Use the Down arrow to Attack, swinging Kuros' sword.

Select: Enters Demo or Continue Mode.

Start/Attack: Starts the game, swings Kuros' sword, or restarts the game in the Continue Mode.

Sound On/Off: A "toggle" switch that will turn the sound effects off when pressed during play; press the button again to turn the sound back on.

Reset: If the game malfunctions, press the tiny ACL button with the tip of a pen or a toothpick. Pressing this button will also erase the electronic record of the previous high score. Note that the game will likely begin to act unpredictably as battery power runs out.

NUMBER OF WORLDS:

There are seven stages of actions.

NUMBER OF LIVES:

You will start the game with 19 Life Units, losing one each time you are successfully attacked by the enemy. The game is over when you have lost all of your lives.

ON/OFF

There is no on/off switch for the game. Instead, the game will automatically turn itself off three or four minutes after the last button has been pushed.

If you are going to be putting your game away for a few months, it would probably be best to remove the batteries to eliminate the possibility of leakage.

Removing or replacing the batteries will erase the record of the highest score.

HOW TO CAPTURE THE BEASTIES

Use your sword to destroy the bats and eventually Malkil. You'll have to avoid the fireballs, killer bees and deadly spiders, since none of these can be destroyed.

Move quickly to collect the magic keys and diamonds when they appear on screen. When you have three keys, the rusty gate protecting the evil wizard disappear.

When the wizard has been destroyed, a Victory message will appear, and a special melody will be played before you move into the next stage of the game.

SCORING POINTS

The system will display your current and highest score on screen. The highest number the counter can display is 99,900 points; if you manage to beat this score, the counter will return to zero, but the last two zeros will flash continuously to indicate that you have "rolled over" the score. This allows the most intrepid Wizards & Warriors player to score as many as 199,800 points in one session.

Here are the available points:

Destroying a bat. 100 points.
Attacking the wizard. 200 points.
Grabbing a key. 200 points.
Grabbing a diamond. 800 points.
Completing a stage. 1,000 points.

POWER ZOOMING

When the game is over, press the Select button to enter the Continue mode. The word CON will appear on the scoreboard.

To restart at the last stage you reached, press the Start button. The score will be reset to 0 and Life Units to 19.

Another way to continue the game is to press the Select button to exit the Continue mode and enter the Demo mode. Press Start to begin a new game.

WWF WrestleMania Challenge

There's a lot going on in this little handheld contest. Three rings are displayed, one above the other.

To complete a round, you must overcome Big Boss Man in ring #1 and grab the hidden key, climb the ladder to ring #2 and beat Andre the Giant and grab the key there, and then climb the ladder to the topmost ring and defeat "Macho Man" Randy Savage there.

Up in the top ring you see poor Miss Elizabeth, chained down and guarded by the Macho Man. While you're fighting on a lower level, your opponents are stalking you from above.

There are a total of 20 rounds of increasing difficulty available, and you can choose between a Beginner or Advanced level of play.

MANUFACTURER: Acclaim Entertainment

CHARACTERS
You are Hulk Hogan, the Hulkster himself, in a three-ring battle to free Miss Elizabeth.

CONTROL PAD
Arrows: The arrows will move the Hulkster Left or Right on each of the three levels of the contest. When the ladder isavailable, press the Up arrow to climb, or the Down arrow to descent.

Select: Used to select skill levels, the Demo mode or to enter the Continue mode.

Start/Wrestle: Starts the game or restarts the game in Continue mode.

Sound On/Off: Press the button to turn the sound and music off; press the button again to resume the din.

Reset: If the game malfunctions, press the tiny ACL button with the tip of a pen or a toothpick. Pressing this button will also erase the electronic record of the previous high score. Note that the game will likely begin to act unpredictably as battery power runs out.

COLLECTING A KEY
To snag one of the keys to the release of Miss Elizabeth, press the Start/Wrestle button to make Hulk jump and then press the Up button to grab the key. When you have collected one, you will see a key displayed at the top of the screen.

NUMBER OF LIVES

You start the game with three lives; each time you are defeated by an opponent, you will lose one life.

ON/OFF

There is no on/off switch for the game. Instead, the game will automatically turn itself off three or four minutes after the last button has been pushed.

If you are going to be putting your game away for a few months, it would probably be best to remove the batteries to eliminate the possibility of leakage.

Removing or replacing the batteries will erase the record of the highest score.

SCORING POINTS:

After all that work, here's what you'll earn:

100 points for overpowering Big Boss Man or Andre the Giant.
200 points for collecting a key.
300 points for besting "Macho Man" Randy Savage.
1,000 points for rescuing Miss Elizabeth and completing a round.

The maximum score that can be displayed on the screen is 99,900 points. If you get past that score (really?) the scoreboard will return to 0 and the last two zeros will flash continuously, allowing you the chance to score a total of 199,800 points.

CONTINUE

When the game ends, press the Select button to continue the game.

If you press the Start button, you will resume play at the last round you reached in the game just ended, with a score of 0.

If you press the Select button again to exit the Continue mode, you can start over again (press Select again to change to skill level L1 or L2) and then press Start.

·7·
Konami

C

Oh say, can you C? This is the latest version of one of the most successful electronic shoot-em-ups. This is "C" as in "Contra," which has had an exceptionally long run as an arcade game and in PC and Nintendo versions.

The dedicated handheld version offered by Konami puts you in control of Mad Dog, a courageous member of the Special Forces Elite Commando Squad in what is billed as "the ultimate test for the ultimate guerilla warrior."

It seems that not just the Earth but the entire universe that we know and love is poised on the edge of total destruction because of the attack of the "vile alien warmonger Red Falcon."

You'll fight against Red Falcon inside the Death Trap Arena, an enclosed room packed with aliens and guards. Your goal is to blast your way through the attackers and make it to the Falcon Phaso-Sensors at the upper right corner of the screen. You'll move Mad Dog left and right while firing his machine gun at the oncoming swarm.

MANUFACTURER: Konami

CHARACTERS

You are Mad Dog, guerilla fighter, in battle against Red Falcon and his Royal Scum Guard and other defenders.

CONTROL PAD

Arrows: Moves Mad Dog left or right into firing positions.
Select: Button not used in this game.

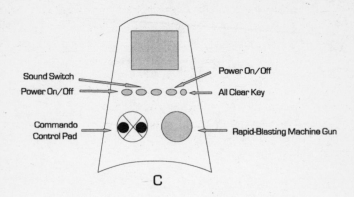

C

Trigger: The right button is used to fire the Rapid-Blasting Machine Gun, firing alien-piercing bullets.

Sound On/Off: Press the Sound Switch to turn the sounds and music off; press the button again to turn the noise, err, music back on.

Reset: If the screen becomes locked (sometimes caused by dying batteries) or after you have changed the batteries, press the tiny All Clear with the point of a pin or toothpick to reset the game.

STARTING THE GAME

Press the On/Start button to bring Mad Dog into Red Falcon's Death Trap Arena. When Mad Dog appears, press the On/Start button a second time to start the game.

SCREEN DISPLAY

At the top left corner of the screen you will see a display of the distance between Mad Dog and his goal, the Phaso-Sensors.

At the bottom right corner of the screen you will see a combined display of the current stage, the number of surviving Mad Dog commandos and the score.

NUMBER OF WORLDS

There are three versions of the same Death Trap Arena scene, each one more difficult than the one before. Once you clear a stage, you will have to destroy a final Falcon Phaso-Sensor in order to move on to the next stage.

You will save the world and the universe if you can clear three stages.

NUMBER OF LIVES

You will start the contest with a total of four lives. Each time Mad Dog is hit by an alien cannon shell or touched by one of Red Falcon's guards, he will lose a life.

ON/OFF

Press the Power Off switch to turn off the game. You will erase the high score for the current game when you do so.

C is a trademark of Konami Inc. Handheld game © 1989 Konami Inc.

Double Dribble

This is "in your face" basketball. You're playing against this short, lightweight little computer trying to score as many points as possible in four timed quarters.

You are always on the offense, trying to sink baskets from way outside, in the lane or a tricky slam dunk up close. Each quarter lasts for 120 seconds of real time, although you will lose seconds from the clock if the ball is stolen or you miss a shot.

MANUFACTURER: Konami

CHARACTERS

It's you against the computer. If you choose a 2-player game, you and a friend will take turns alternating quarters until both have played four quarters. The computer will play defense in all games.

CONTROL PAD

Arrows: Moves your player Up, Down, Left or Right to one of 11 predefined court positions. You can shoot from the 8 most inside positions. You can move the ball up the court vertically or horizontally, but not on a diagonal.

Shooting: To launch the ball toward the basket, press the Shoot/Player Select pad.

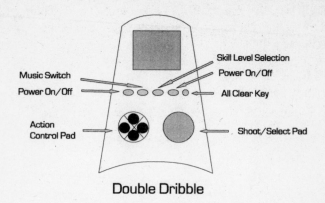

Double Dribble

Select: Press the button to choose between the three levels of play. The first level is High School, with two defenders. The second level is College and the third level is Pro, each presents three defenders.

Sound On/Off: Press the Music switch once to turn the music off; press the button again to resume the entertainment.

Reset: If the screen becomes locked or if you need to clear the scores, press the tiny All Clear button with the point of a pin or a toothpick.

TIMING

Each quarter lasts 120 seconds, with the clock running at real time. However, any time a defender steals the ball it will cost you 6 seconds and send you back to the J (farthest out) position. You will also lose 5 seconds from the clock each time you miss a shot.

ON/OFF

Press the Power Off switch to turn the game off.

SCORING POINTS

The highest score in this game is earned by a successful slam dunk, which gives 5 points if you can make it to the A position directly below the basket; you'll have just 1 second to get into the air and ram home the ball. If your hang time is more than 1 second, you will miss your shot and be sent back to the J position to try again.

You can see the shooting positions in the accompanying drawing.

You'll pick up 2 points if you can sink a basket from B, C, D or E, the four inner positions in and around the hoop.

Double Dribble

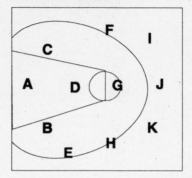

There is 1 point to be had from a successful shot from the F, G or H positions at the top of the key.

You cannot shoot from the outermost I, J or K positions.

The highest number of points that can be displayed on the scoreboard is 200; if you reach that level, the score will recycle to 0 and start over from there.

Gradius

Your goal is to Vipe out the Bacterions. Can you make the grade?

In this arcade hit, you're out to attempt to defend your home planet Gradius and its millions of innocent citizens from the attack of the Bacterion forces. You are armed with super-duper Plutonic Lasers.

MANUFACTURER: Konami

CHARACTERS
You, yourself and you, at the controls of your very own Vic Viper fighter.

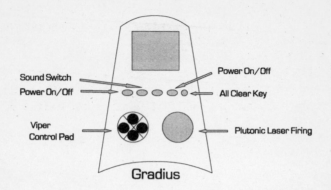

Gradius

CONTROL PAD

Arrows: Move the Vic Viper up or down on the screen.

Trigger: Press the fire button on the right side of the handheld unit to launch Plutonic Lasers.

Select: Button not used in this game.

Start: Press the On/Start button to begin the game.

Sound On/Off: Press the Sound switch once to turn off the sound effects and music; press the button again to turn the sound back on.

Reset: To unlock the screen or erase the currently recorded high score, press the tiny All Clear button using a pin or toothpick.

NUMBER OF WORLDS

There are four levels to the game, with the fighting becoming more and more difficult with each advanced stage. In order to move on to a later stage, you'll have to destroy the Big Core at the end of each challenge.

NUMBER OF LIVES

You'll start the game with four Vic Vipers. For each 6,000 points scored, you'll earn another Viper. Each time you fail to destroy an attacking Bacterion Fighter, you'll lose points on your Force Meter; when all of the points are gone, you will lose one of your lives. If you are hit by a missile, crystal or an enemy fighter itself, you will lose all of the points on the meter and forfeit a life.

ON/OFF

Press the Power Off switch to turn off the game.

ENEMIES

There are four types of opponents: Bacterion Fighters and Big Cores are no match for your Plutonic Laser. Carnage Crystals and Floating Continents, though, are indestructible.

SCORING POINTS

Each Bacterion fighter you shoot down is worth 20 points. Deadly Big Cores which appear at the end of each level are worth 400 points each.

Gradius is a trademark of Konami Inc. Handheld game © 1989 Konami Inc.

Skate or Die

They don't make much of an attempt to put a story line on this version of the Skate or Die series, downscaled to fit into a handheld unit from Konami.

Your entire being is to be concentrated on getting from the beginning to the end of a four-stage skateboarder's dream (or is it a nightmare?) of a track called the Psycho Path (get it?).

You'll race against time, avoiding obstacles such as Wally's Wall, the Slip 'N Slide Oil Slick, The Hole Thing, the Carnivorous Crevice and Border Guards.

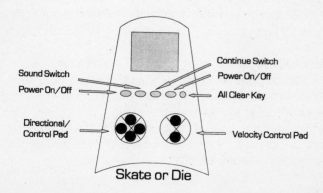

Skate or Die

The only way to win this race is to make it to the finish flag before the Time Limit expires. While you're zizzing and snagging left, right, up and down, keep an eye on the Miles to Go Meter to get some idea of how much farther you have to go to finish a stage.

MANUFACTURER: Konami

CHARACTERS: It's you, skating or dying.

CONTROL PAD

Arrows: Push the Left or Right arrow button to move in one of those directions; push the Up arrow to jump up in the air.

Velocity: The right button on the handheld unit is the Velocity Control Pad. Push the Up arrow to increase your speed; press the Down arrow to slow down.

Start: To begin the game, press the On/Start button. The screen will

Sound On/Off: Press the Sound Switch to turn the sound and music off; press the button again to resume the din.

Reset: To clear the screen if it is locked or to clear out high scores, press the tiny All Clear key with the point of a pin or a toothpick,

NUMBER OF WORLDS

There are four, count 'em Psychopathic Stages in the game. The scenery is the same for each of them, but the obstacles tend to come faster and closer together.

NUMBER OF LIVES

The bad news is that you've got only one life to give for skateboarding. The good news is that you have unlimited Continues.

CONTINUE

On this handheld game, the center button is called the Continue switch. If the Time Limit runs out and your game is over, press the Continue button and you will be brought back to life at the beginning of the Psychopathic Stage where you died.

The Continue switch is also the doorway to the special set of Bonus Paths hidden in the game. Once you have survived all four levels, press the Continue switch and then the On/Start button.

ON/OFF

Press the Power Off switch to turn off the game.

Teenage Mutant Ninja Turtles

Turtles in a half shell, in trouble again, this time in a handheld three-in-one challenge. Yes, that's right: there are no less than three different games in this little package from Konami.

Once again, you are one of the good turtles, out to rescue poor April O'Neil, who has once again been kidnapped by the evil Shredder. You've got to rescue her before Shredder succeeds in brainwashing her as a member of his Ninjitsu Foot Clan. April is held inside Shredder's Asylum, a glass container that is protected by Houdini's Escape-Proof Lock and Chain.

In Game 1 (clever name, huh?) you've got the simplest challenge. You will have to battle your way past oncoming nasties and make it into the water, find the hidden Freedom Key and then unlock April's chains. Watch out for the creatures in the water, while you're at it.

In Game 2, you'll also have to get into the water, but first you'll have to retrieve a set of special bombs and set them off around Shredder's Asylum until the screen is blown away. Be careful, now! Putting the boomers in the wrong place could result in vaporizing poor April, and that's not all that clever. Once the shield has been taken down, you'll have to go back into the water to find the Freedom Key, hidden in one of several boxes. Oh, by the way: do all of this quickly, before time runs out.

Game 3 is just like Game 2, only faster and more treacherous. Yipes!

MANUFACTURER: Konami

CHARACTERS

You are one of the heroic Teenage Mutant Ninja Turtles, out to do battle against Shredder and his minions (including Mouser and Flap Jaws) to rescue sweet April, held captive once more.

CONTROL PAD

Arrows: The Turtle Control Button (left button) is used to move your turtle Up, Down, Left or Right on the screen.

The Slice and Dice Button: The right button is a multi-purpose fighting control. Press the Left side of the button to swing the razor-sharp Katana Blade. Press the Right side of the button to throw a karate chop.

You will also use the Slice and Dice button to open the boxes you discover beneath the water in search of the hidden Freedom Key.

Select: Chooses between Game 1, 2 or 3.

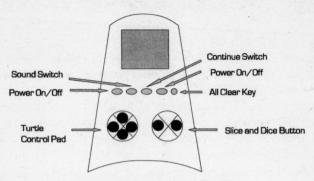

Sound Switch

Power On/Off

Continue Switch

Power On/Off

All Clear Key

Turtle
Control Pad

Slice and Dice Button

Teenage Mutant Ninja Turtles

Start: To begin the game press the On/Start button to turn on the power.

Sound On/Off: Press the Sound Switch to turn off the sound effects and music; press the button again to turn the clatter back on.

Reset: To clear the screen or reset the game if it becomes locked, press the tiny All Clear button with the end of a pin or toothpick.

NUMBER OF LIVES

You have a total of three lives to expend on behalf of April. You will lose lives if you are touched by the Shredder Shuriken (a throwing star) or by one of Shredder's unpleasant friends, Mouser or Flap Jaws or if you bump into the underwater hazards including the Great Electro-Barrier Reef or the Pizza/Turtle Cutter.

ON/OFF

Press the Power Off switch to turn off the game.

Top Gun

There you are, soaring high above a flotilla of cruisers and carriers, defending the skies against any intruder. You've got your high-tech, high-speed F-14 jet fighter; you've got a full load of air-to-air and air-to-surface heat-seeking missiles; you've got this neat leather jacket and rad reflective sunglasses and you've got one huge movie star contract in your pocket. You're Top Gun!

MANUFACTURER: Konami

CHARACTERS You, Top Gun.

NUMBER OF PLAYERS
1 or 2. In two-player game, contestants will alternate play.

CONTROL PAD
Arrows: Move your fighter Up, Down, Left to Right on the screen. What you will see on the screen will be

Select: Used to select between 1-player and 2-player games.

Trigger: Used to launch Air-to-Air and Air-to-Surface Heat Seeking Missiles.

Sound On/Off: Press the Sound switch to turn off the sounds and music; press the button again to restore the noise.

Reset: To reset the game when the screen is locked, or after batteries have been changed, press the tiny All-Clear button with a pin or toothpick.

NUMBER OF WORLDS
To win the game you must survive three missions, but you can't just lay back and hide. Every 90 seconds—if you're still flying—the game will move into a new and more advanced zone.

NUMBER OF LIVES
You'll begin the contest with three supersonic Naval F-14 fighters. When all three are gone, the game is over. Each time you fail to shoot down a threatening enemy plane, ship or missile, a section of your Energy Gauge will be taken away; points on the gauge will also automatically be

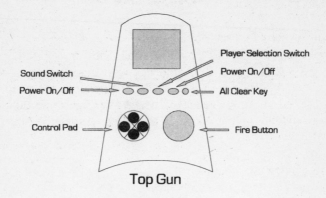

Top Gun

reduced by one point for each 16 seconds of play. When all of the points are gone, you will lose one of your fighters.

ON/OFF
Press the Power Off switch to turn off the game.

HOW TO SHOOT DOWN THE BOGEYS
Line up your target in the cross hairs of the missile sight. At one point in its movement across the screen, the enemy will flash three times; he is most vulnerable during his second and third flash.

SCORING POINTS
You'll earn 10 points for each Scavenger Fighter knocked down, 30 points for each Anti-Peacekeeping Battle Cruiser destroyed and 100 points for every Death-Tipped Missile blown away.

The top score for a Top Gun is 19,990 points; if you every get up this high, the score will reset back to 0 and go on from there.

Announcing the Ultimate Insider Newsletter!

Want more inside information like you've found in this book?

Want honest and impartial reviews that are not sponsored by *you-know-who?*

Want it delivered every month to your mailbox?

You'll stay *months* ahead of the magazines. You'll learn about new game paks as soon as they are announced, before your local dealers have even heard of the games. You'll read the latest, greatest hints and strategies from the Nintendo game experts all around the country! You'll learn how to build the Ultimate System!

Each 8- to 12-page newsletter, written by the authors of this book, will be packed with solid information like you've found in this book. Plus, we'll present interviews with game counselors about their favorite strategies. We'll talk to game designers about how—and why—they do what they do.

You'll be eligible for exciting contests with prizes including free game paks of the hottest new titles. You can also expect special offers from manufacturers with discounts on their merchandise.

And, you'll be the first to know about the exciting details of the next volume of *Ultimate Unauthorized Nintendo Game Strategies* and other publications from Bantam Books.

Now here's the best news: The regular price for all of this is only $19.95 a year! But even better: Readers of this book can subscribe for just $17.95 for 12 issues. That's less than $1.50 an issue. (See coupon for prices for our Canadian friends.)

Fill out your name and address carefully and send $17.95 in check or money order for 12 issues of the Ultimate Insider Newsletter. Make checks payable to Ultimate Insider.

Ultimate Insider Newsletter is published by Word Association, Inc., P.O. Box 6093, Holliston, MA 01746. It is in no way endorsed by or related to Bantam Books or Nintendo of America Inc.

— —

Ultimate Insider Newsletter
P.O. Box 6093
Holliston, MA 01746

Enclosed is $17.95 in check or money order for 12 issues. Canadian subscribers please send $20.95 U.S. funds or $25.95 Canadian funds.

Name: _____

Address: _____

City: _____ State: _____ Zip: _____

FREE MEMBERSHIP
The Puzzle Game
to CHEWS!

Mail in this card for your free membership to
SETA's QBILLION Club
(A 4.95 VALUE)

With your free membership you will receive these items:

- **FREE club gifts and contest information!**
- **THE SETA CONTROL PAD (monthly newsletter).**
- **QBILLION MEMBERSHIP CARD.**
- **THE QBILLION PUZZLE SOLVING LANGUAGE MANUAL.**

Name_____ Age_____

Address_____

City_____State_____Zip_____

Do you own a GAMEBOY? Yes____ No____

How many games do you own?_____

SETA U.S.A., Inc.
105 E. Reno Ave., Ste. 22 • Las Vegas, NV 89119
ATTN: QBILLION CLUB
(702)-795-7996

PUTTING THIS CARD IN OUR HANDS COULD PUT A FREE KONAMI GAME IN YOURS.

You'll receive the Konami game of your choice if your name is chosen in our monthly drawing. Simply fill out this card and drop it in the mail. No purchase necessary.

Each entry card qualifies for one monthly drawing. Please fill in all information or include all information on a 3 x 5 card and mail to: Konami Inc., P.O. Box 11210, Chicago, IL 60611-0210.

One entry per person. Winner will be notified by mail within 30 days of drawing. This contest void in Washington, Missouri, Florida, Ohio and other places where prohibited. In Kansas, a cash alternative in lieu of a prize may be requested. This contest may be terminated without notice.

Name_____

Street_____ Apt #_____

City_____ State_____ Zip Code_____

Phone #_(_____)_____ Age_____

READY FOR ANOTHER CHALLENGE?

IF YOU'VE MASTERED THE GAMES IN **ULTIMATE UNAUTHORIZED NINTENDO® GAME BOY™ STRATEGIES** AND WANT "INSIDE" TIPS, TRICKS, AND NEVER-BEFORE-PUBLISHED INFORMATION ON TODAY'S HOT GAMES FOR THE NINTENDO ENTERTAINMENT SYSTEM®, DON'T MISS VOLUMES 1 AND 2 OF **ULTIMATE UNAUTHORIZED NINTENDO® GAME STRATEGIES**, FEATURING:

VOLUME 1:
Double Dragon II: The Revenge™, Ultima™, Jordan vs. Bird™, MegaMan 2™, Cybernoid™, Air Fortress™, Super Mario Bros.®, Super Mario Bros. 2™, and Legend of Zelda®. It also covers hot peripherals like the Game Boy™ portable system, and the U-Force™ and Power Glove™ controllers.

VOLUME 2:
Teenage Mutant Ninja Turtles®, DuckTales™, Amagon™, Boy and His Blob™, Casino Kid™, Ninja Gaiden™, Paper Boy™, Baseball Simulator 1.000™, Willow™, Bases Loaded II™, Super Mario Land™, and instructions for building the ultimate Nintendo®game system with hi-fi sound and big screen video!

Available at your local computer book retailer, or order directly from Bantam Books.To order now, fill out the coupon below. Please add $4.00 for shipping and handling.

- -

34892-2   ULTIMATE UNAUTHORIZED NINTENDO®
GAME STRATEGIES, VOLUME 1, $9.95
QTY ___ X $9.95 = $_____

34934-1   ULTIMATE UNAUTHORIZED NINTENDO®
GAME STRATEGIES, VOLUME 2, $9.95
QTY ___ X $9.95 = $_____
+ shipping and handling $ 4.00
TOTAL PRICE $_____

NAME_____

ADDRESS_____

CITY_____STATE_____ZIP_____

Send your order to:
Bantam Books, Dept NN, 414 East Golf Road, Des Plaines, IL 60016

Nintendo® is a registered trademark of Nintendo of America Inc.These books are not authorized or endorsed by Nintendo of America Inc.